English

轻松说英语

（下册）

U0117227

即刻扫码

1. 配套音频
聆听音频资源，提升英语语感

2. 词汇积累
积累实用词汇，打好英语基础

3. 文化交流
感受文化魅力，增强学习兴趣

4. 课后互动
"晒"出学习成果，交流学习心得

上海教育出版社
SHANGHAI EDUCATIONAL
PUBLISHING HOUSE

图书在版编目（CIP）数据

　轻松说英语. 下册 / 魏祖洪，叶晗修主编. — 上海：
上海教育出版社，2024.8. — ISBN 978-7-5720-2696-6

　Ⅰ. H319.9

　中国国家版本馆CIP数据核字第2024FG0028号

责任编辑　赵忠卫　杜金丹
特约审稿　冯　豪
封面设计　王　捷

轻松说英语　下册
魏祖洪　叶晗修　主编

出版发行　上海教育出版社有限公司
官　　网　www.seph.com.cn
地　　址　上海市闵行区号景路159弄C座
邮　　编　201101
印　　刷　上海叶大印务发展有限公司
开　　本　787×1092　1/16　印张 13.75
字　　数　175 千字
版　　次　2024年8月第1版
印　　次　2024年8月第1次印刷
书　　号　ISBN 978-7-5720-2696-6/G·2378
定　　价　45.00 元

如发现质量问题，读者可向本社调换　电话：021-64373213

老年大学英语口语系列教材编委会

主　任　熊仿杰

副主任　黄建辉

总策划　赵忠卫

编　委　（按姓氏笔画排序）

王秀珍　王凤英　王道英　马丽娟　方帼萍

叶晗修　冯　豪　朱多林　朱建全　闫守来

汤可发　杜金丹　李　克　吴粉华　张　浩

张咏梅　张琪安　武月娟　郐立立　施晓征

徐中一　盛晨晨　董启梅　曾如刚　蔡淑萍

魏　翔　魏祖洪

《轻松说英语》编写组

主　编　魏祖洪

执行主编　叶晗修

组　员　盛晨晨　王凤英

　　　　　吴粉华　武月娟

编写说明

"老年大学英语口语系列教材"整套分初、中、高三个层级,分别为《开口说英语》《轻松说英语》《流利说英语》。每个层级的教材学制均为一年,全套教材共三年学完。

参与"老年大学英语口语系列教材"编写的老年大学共有 10 所,共选派了 14 位优秀的一线教师参编,名单如下:

上海老年大学	王道英	副教授		
无锡市老年大学	魏祖洪	副译审		
苏州市老年大学	董启梅	中学高级	闫守来	中学高级
金陵老年大学	武月娟	中学高级	郇立立	本科学历
镇江市老年大学	张琪安	副教授		
常州老年大学	吴粉华	高级讲师	张咏梅	中学高级
芜湖老年大学	盛晨晨	中学一级		
江苏青春老年大学	王凤英	副教授	朱建全	中学高级
绍兴市老年大学	曾如刚	副教授		
厦门老年大学	蔡淑萍	副教授		

"老年大学英语口语系列教材"编委会由三部分成员组成:一是全体参编教师;二是参编学校对教材编写起推动、领导和组织作用的校长、教务主任或系主任;三是上海教育出版社负责教材出版的编辑和相关审稿人员。

为了使三个层级的教材具有统一的编辑思路和较高的编校质量,上海教育出版社由赵忠卫(副编审)、杜金丹(编辑)、叶晗修(副教授)、冯豪(硕士、高级口译)组成编辑审稿小组,负责整套教材的编辑

1

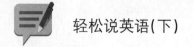

加工和审稿工作。

三个层级的教材各自成立编写组。其中,《轻松说英语》编写组由 魏祖洪 、武月娟、王凤英、吴粉华、盛晨晨组成,由 魏祖洪 任主编。由于 魏祖洪 老师的健康原因,特增补上海市徐汇区老年大学的叶晗修副教授参加编写组,并担任上册的副主编、下册的执行主编,来完成《轻松说英语》全部初稿的整理、修改、统稿和校样审读等工作。

《轻松说英语》上下册初稿写作分工情况如下:

魏祖洪　　上册:第 1、2、7 单元;下册:第 14 单元。

王凤英　　上册:第 3、4、5、6、8、9 单元。

盛晨晨　　上册:第 10、11、12、13、14、15 单元;下册:第 1 单元。

吴粉华　　下册:第 2、3、4、5、6、7、8 单元。

武月娟　　下册:第 9、10、11、12、13、15 单元。

"老年大学英语口语系列教材"的主题是"出国探亲和旅游",用大话题统领小话题的方式来安排三个层级教材每个单元的内容。所要达到的目标是整套教材全部小话题的集合能较完整地反映"出国探亲和旅游"这个主题。为了适应老年人的学习特点和记忆特点,虽然三个层级教材的主题相同,但内容深度和语言难度则采用螺旋上升的方法进行安排,使前一层级的学习为后一层级的学习在内容上做铺垫,在语言的知识点和难度上打基础。因此,循序渐进地使用这套教材能取得良好的教学效果。

因编者水平有限,书中难免有疏漏之处,恳请广大读者不吝赐教,也期待更多的有识之士能和我们一起参与老年教材的编写工作。

编者

2024 年 6 月

目　　录

Unit 1　Visiting Scenic Spots
参观景点

Ⅰ. Entry and Exit　出入口标识

1. Dialogues　对话

A＝Kim 金姆；B＝Leon 利昂

A：Now we are here in Disneyland. It seems that we are back to childhood again.　我们现在位于迪士尼乐园。我们好像又回到了孩童时代。

B：Look at those excited adults on the rides! They look like children that never grow up.　看那些在游乐设施上玩得那么开心的成年人,他们真是一群长不大的孩子。

A：Yeah，let's follow the map and go to the roller coaster first. It only takes ten minutes in line.　是啊,我们还是跟着地图走,先去坐过山车吧,只需要排队 10 分钟。

B：I dare not ride the roller coaster.　我不敢坐过山车。

A：That was when you were a kid. You can find Disney characters all over the roller coaster. Come on，have a try. Come this way.　那是您小时候的事了,坐过山车时随处都能发现迪士尼人物。来吧,您可以的。这边走。

B：Fine.　好的。

1

(Ladies and gentlemen, please fasten your belts. Do remember that you may not stand up before it stops. 女士们,先生们,请系紧安全带,一定要记住过山车停下之前不要站起来。)

B: It drives me crazy. Really exciting. 我简直要疯了,实在太刺激了。

A: It's a good experience, isn't it? Now what is the next one? 一次难得的经历,不是吗? 我们接下来玩什么?

B: Let's try some milder rides. I will ride the ferris wheel. I've always found it romantic. 让我们玩些温和的游乐设施吧。我要坐摩天轮,我一直觉得它很浪漫。

A: I am keen on it too. The ferris wheel goes up and down, just like the lives. 我也很喜欢。摩天轮的高低起伏,就像我们的人生。

2. Words and Expressions 单词和词组

(1) entry /'entrɪ/ n. 进入,入口,条目

(2) exit /'eksɪt/ n. 出口,退场

(3) ride /raɪd/ n. 游乐设施

(4) roller /'rəulə/ n. [机]滚筒,滚转机

(5) coaster /'kəustə/ n. 雪橇,杯托,小托盘

(6) roller coaster 过山车

(7) dare /deə(r)/ v. & n. 胆敢,挑战

(8) characters /'kærɪktəz/ n. 特性,人物角色(character 的复数)

(9) mild /maɪld/ adj. 温和的,轻微的

(10) Ferris /'ferɪs/ n. 费里斯(人名)

（11）wheel　/wiːl/　*n*.　轮子

（12）ferris wheel　摩天轮

（13）romantic　/rəʊ'mæntɪk/　*adj*.　浪漫的

3. Tips and Notes　要点解释

（1）I dare not ride the roller coaster.　我不敢坐过山车。

I dare not …等同于 I am afraid of …，表达对坐过山车有畏惧的情绪。

（2）Do remember that you may not stand up before it stops. 一定要记住过山车停下之前不要站起来。

这里的 Do 并不是助动词或者行为动词，而是起强调作用。

（3）I am keen on it too.　我也很喜欢。

be keen on …类似于 like sth. very much，表达热衷于做某事。

4. Drills　句型操练

（1）It seems that …

It seems that he understands the text.

Now it seems that I have become one of them.

It seems that cats have replaced dogs as the most popular pets in American homes.

（2）I dare not …

I dare not go there.

I dare not think of the car accident.

I dare not speak English in public.

（3）No wonder …

No wonder we love this guy.

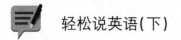

No wonder you always do well.

No wonder they often have lunch together.

5. Recitation 常用句背诵

（1）It seems that we are back to childhood again. 我们好像又回到了孩童时代。

（2）I dare not ride the roller coaster. 我不敢坐过山车。

（3）Let's try some milder rides. 让我们玩些温和的游乐设施吧。

6. Follow Up 拓展学习

Universal Studios

Universal Studios is located in the northwest suburbs of downtown Los Angeles. At the beginning of the 20th century, filmmakers found the ideal filming natural environment，making this land gradually become a world-famous studio. In 1908，Hollywood produced one of the earliest feature films，*The Enemy of Monte Cristo*. The 1930s and 1940s were the director's heyday, producing a large number of outstanding films that became representative of the history of films，and the influence of American films throughout the world. Universal Studios is an amusement park that recreates the themes of movies, with games featuring several big-name movies most popular，such as *Shrek* 4D Movie，*The Mummy's Revenge*，*The Jurassic Park* and *The Devil Terminator* and so on. Universal Studios，World Carnival and Disneyland are the most three famous themes in the world.

好莱坞环球影城

　　好莱坞环球影城位于洛杉矶市区西北郊。20 世纪初,电影制片商在此发现理想的拍片自然环境,使这块土地逐渐成为世界闻名的影城。1908 年,好莱坞拍出了早期的故事片之一《基督山恩仇记》。20 世纪三四十年代是好莱坞的鼎盛时期,摄制了大量成为电影史上代表作的优秀影片,并使美国电影的影响遍及世界。好莱坞环球影城是一个再现电影主题的游乐园,其中以多部大制作电影为主题的景点最受欢迎。例如,《怪物史瑞克》(4D 电影)、《木乃伊归来》、《侏罗纪公园》、《终结者》等。环球影城、环球嘉年华和迪士尼主题乐园并称为世界三大娱乐主题乐园。

Ⅱ. Tips for Visiting　参观注意事项

1. Dialogues　对话

A＝Visitor 参观者；B＝Staff 工作人员

A：Excuse me. I wonder if there will be any exhibition next week.　劳驾,我想咨询一下下周有什么展览。

B：We have Renaissance art exhibition next Friday.　下周五我们有文艺复兴时期的艺术展。

A：Do I need an appointment?　请问需要预约吗?

B：Yes, you can fill out the registration form now.　是的,您现在可以填写表格登记预约。

A：OK, how much is the admission?　好的,门票是多少钱?

B：180 RMB per person.　180 元/人。

A：Fine. What's the most striking works in this exhibition?　好的。这次展览中令人惊艳的展品有哪些?

B：We will show works by Michelangelo，Raphael and Da Vinci. These artifacts are hundreds of years old. 我们会展出米开朗基罗、拉斐尔以及达·芬奇的作品。这些作品距今都有几百年的历史了。

A：Great，I don't know much about western painting，but I'm interested in statues. By the way，may I take photos in the museum？ 太好了，虽然我不太了解西方油画，但我对雕像很感兴趣。我可以在馆内拍照吗？

B：I'm sorry, sir. We don't take photos in the museum. Drinks are also not allowed inside. There is a lounge area for drinks. 不好意思，先生，馆内严禁拍照。另外，饮料也不能带入馆内。馆内设有休息区，会提供饮料。

A：OK. Is there a souvenir shop？ 好的，馆内有纪念品商店吗？

B：Yes，sir. We have a souvenir shop at the end of each section. 有的，先生。我们在每个展区的末端都设有纪念品商店。

A：That's great. What time will the exhibition begin？ 那可真好。展览从什么时间开始？

B：At nine in the morning. 早上九点就开始了。

A：Got it. Thank you so much. 好的，谢谢您。

B：You're welcome. 不客气。

2. Words and Expressions 单词和词组

（1）exhibition ／ˌeksɪˈbɪʃən／ *n*. 展览，展览会，展览品

（2）Renaissance ／rɪˈneɪs(ə)ns／ *n*. 文艺复兴(时期)

（3）fill out 填写(表格等)

（4）registration ／ˌredʒɪˈstreɪʃən／ *n*. 登记，注册，挂号

（5）admission /əd'mɪʃən/ *n*. 入场费,进入许可,录用

（6）striking /'straɪkɪŋ/ *adj*. 显著的,突出的,惊人的

（7）artifact /'ɑːtɪfækt/ *n*. 人工制品,手工艺品

（8）statue /'stætʃuː/ *n*. 雕像

（9）lounge /laʊndʒ/ *n*. 休息室,闲逛,躺椅,(英)酒吧

（10）souvenir /ˌsuːvə'nɪə(r)/ *n*. 纪念品,礼物

3. Tips and Notes 要点解释

（1）180 RMB per person 180元/人

原句等同于 180 RMB for one person,per 等同于 for one。

（2）We will show works by Michelangelo，Raphael and Da Vinci. 我们会展出米开朗基罗、拉斐尔以及达·芬奇的作品。

works by ...后跟作者,而 works of ...后跟作品内容。

（3）We don't take photos in the museum. 馆内严禁拍照。

We don't take photos ... 可以和 We don't allow to take photos ...进行替换,表达禁止拍照。

4. Drills 句型操练

（1）I wonder if ...

I wonder if you are well.

I wonder if you have friends.

I wonder if I should tell her the truth.

（2）at the end of ...

I want them back at the end of the lesson.

His voice dropped at the end of the sentence.

You can see a bank at the end of the street.

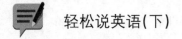

(3) I love …

I love what I do.

I love everything about you.

I love doing challenging things.

5. Recitation　常用句背诵

(1) I wonder if there will be any exhibition next week.　我想咨询一下下周有什么展览。

(2) We don't take photos in the museum.　馆内严禁拍照。

6. Follow Up　拓展学习

The Renaissance

The Renaissance refers to a European ideological and cultural movement that took place between the 14th century and the 16th century, reflecting the demands of the emerging bourgeoisie.

The concept of "Renaissance" was used by Italian humanists and scholars from the 14th century to the 16th century. It was thought that literature and art were highly prosperous in the classical times of Greece and Rome, but decayed in the "dark ages" of the Middle Ages, and were not "regenerated" and "revived" until the 14th century, hence the name "Renaissance".

The Renaissance first emerged in Italian cities, and later extended to Western European countries, reached its peak in the 16th century, brought a period of scientific and artistic revolution, opened the beginning of modern European history, is considered to be the boundary between the Middle Ages and modern times. The

Renaissance is one of the three major ideological liberation movements (Renaissance，Reformation and Enlightenment) in western Europe.

文艺复兴

文艺复兴是指发生在 14 世纪至 16 世纪的一场反映欧洲新兴资产阶级要求的思想文化运动。

"文艺复兴"的概念在 14 世纪至 16 世纪时已被意大利的人文主义作家和学者所使用。当时的人们认为，文艺在希腊、罗马古典时代曾高度繁荣，但在中世纪"黑暗时代"却衰败湮没，直到 14 世纪后才获得"再生"与"复兴"，因此称为"文艺复兴"。

文艺复兴最先在意大利各城市兴起，之后扩展到西欧各国，于 16 世纪达到顶峰，是科学与艺术革命时期，揭开了欧洲近代历史的序幕，被认为是中世纪和近代的分界。文艺复兴是西欧近代三大思想解放运动(文艺复兴、宗教改革与启蒙运动)之一。

Ⅲ. Visiting Etiquette　参观礼仪

1. Dialogues　对话

A＝Amy 艾米；B＝Ben 本

A：My friend is going to appear in a musical about mythology.　我朋友要出演一场与神话故事有关的音乐剧。

B：Is Jim the guy learning to sing?　是学习演唱的吉姆吗？

A：Yes，it is him. It's next Friday. Would you like to go with me?　正是他。下周五，您愿意和我一起去吗？

B：Yes，I would like to. Jim has a good sense of humor. I know nothing about musicals. Do I need to dress formally?　我愿意。吉姆很幽默。我对观看音乐剧的要求一无所知。我需要穿得正式一些吗？

A：Take it easy, you could choose the dress to wear that day, as far as I know, the musical needs to be in line half an hour in advance, otherwise we might be in the back row. 轻松点,您可以选择连衣裙,据我所知,观看音乐剧需要提前半个小时去排队,否则我们可能会坐在后排。

B：Yes, I heard that too. Shall I bring drinks or snacks? 是的,我也听说了。可以带饮料或者零食吗?

A：If I were you, I probably wouldn't be carrying these. Musicals should be enjoyed quietly. 如果是我的话,我可能不会携带这些。音乐剧需要静静欣赏。

B：I got it. Can I record it? 好的。我可以录像吗?

A：That's OK. I'm sure Jim would like to see himself on stage. 这个是可以的,我想吉姆肯定也想看一看自己在台上的表现。

B：OK, what else should I pay attention to? 好的,还有什么需要注意的?

A：I think that's all. We're going to have a great evening. 我觉得就这些,我们将会度过一个愉快的夜晚。

2. Words and Expressions　单词和词组

(1) etiquette　/ˈetɪkət/　*n.*　礼节,规矩

(2) appear　/əˈpɪə(r)/　*v.*　出现,显得

(3) mythology　/mɪˈθɒlədʒɪ/　*n.*　神话,神话学,神话集

(4) sense　/sens/　*n.*　感觉,功能;　*v.*　感觉到,检测

(5) formally　/ˈfɔːməlɪ/　*adv.*　正式地,形式上

(6) advance　/ədˈvɑːns/　*v.*　提前,前进;　*n.*　发展

(7) otherwise　/ˈʌðəwaɪz/　*adv.*　否则,另外,在其他方面

10

（8）record /rɪ'kɔːd/ v. 记录，记载

（9）stage /steɪdʒ/ n. 舞台，戏剧； v. 举行，上演，筹划

3. Tips and Notes 要点解释

（1）My friend is going to appear in a musical about mythology. 我朋友要出演一场与神话故事有关的音乐剧。

be going to …是将来时的表达形式之一，用于主观判断，即说话人主观上的计划或者安排。而 will 多用于客观情况，即客观上将要发生的事情。

（2）Is Jim the guy learning to sing? 是学习演唱的吉姆吗？

此处 the guy 是 Jim 的同位语。

（3）I know nothing about musicals. 我对观看音乐剧的要求一无所知。

句意等于 I don't know much about musicals. 其中，nothing 和 not … much 可以互换。

（4）Can I record it? 我可以录像吗？

此处 record 为动词，其读音为/rɪ'kɔːd/，与其为名词时的读音 /'rekɔːd/不相同。

4. Drills 句型操练

（1）as far as …

Not possible，as far as we know.

They walked as far as the others that day.

As far as he told me，he knew nothing about the plan.

（2）… in advance

Thank you for your help in advance.

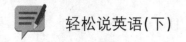

We can prepare some candles in advance.

Thank you for booking hotel rooms for us in advance.

（3）If I were you ...

If I were you，I would not do that.

If I were you，I would go with him.

If I were you，I should give him a lesson.

5. Recitation　常用句背诵

（1）Jim has a good sense of humor.　吉姆很幽默。

（2）Musicals should be enjoyed quietly.　音乐剧需要静静欣赏。

6. Follow Up　拓展学习

Talking about a Vocal Concert　谈论演唱会

A：This is his farewell concert.　这是他的告别演唱会。

B：Are you kidding? Isn't he having the world tour?　您在开玩笑吗？他不是正在进行全球巡回演出吗？

A：He said he's going to retire from singing after the tour.　他说他唱完就"封麦"了。

B：My gosh. No wonder the tickets are so hard to get.　天哪！难怪票那么难买。

A：I'd been listening to his songs in my teenage life.　我从青少年时期就在听他的歌。

B：Me too. I still listen to his songs from time to time.　我也是，时不时还会听他的歌。

Unit 2

手机扫码
听单词和对话

Unit 2　Community Shuttles
社区公交

Ⅰ. Talking about Buses　谈论公交车

1. Dialogues　对话

A＝Visitor 参观者；B＝Local Citizen 当地居民

A：Excuse me，I'm new here. Can you tell me how to get to the nearest supermarket?　打扰一下，我是新来的。您能告诉我怎样去最近的超市吗？

B：Sure. You can take Bus No. 112 and get off at the Times Square.　可以。您可以乘坐 112 路公交车，然后在时代广场下车。

A：Where is the bus stop?　公交车站在哪里？

B：It's a bit far from here. Walk down three blocks and you will find the bus stop.　公交车站离这里有点远。走三个街区，然后您就能找到了。

A：Three blocks? How long will it take to get there?　三个街区吗？那我需要走多长时间？

B：About 40 minutes.　大约 40 分钟。

A：Oh，my gosh. It's too far for me. In China，taking buses is very convenient. We only need to walk for at most 10 minutes to get to the bus stop.　哦，天哪！这对我来说太远了。在中国，乘坐公交车非常方便。我们最多只需要走 10 分钟就可以到达公交车站。

13

B：Sounds great. But it's known to all that there is a huge population in China. I guess every weekday the buses are packed with passengers like a can of sardines. 听起来很棒！但众所周知,中国人口众多,我猜工作日的公交车上挤满了乘客,就像沙丁鱼罐头一样。

A：You have a good imagination. In China most people choose public transportation when going out. 您真有想象力。在中国,大多数人外出时会选择公共交通。

B：It's very common for people here to drive to places where they want to go. Only a few people choose to take buses since they are not so convenient. Besides，the bus fare is not cheap. 在我们国家,人们总是开车去他们想去的地方。因为乘坐公交车不是很便利,而且,车费也不便宜,只有少数人会选择去乘坐。

A：But I know buses here are quite comfortable and nearly every passenger can have a seat. 但是我知道这里的公交车很舒适,几乎每个乘客都有座位。

B：That's true. Each coin has two sides. If you want to experience the bus service in Canada，walk down three blocks and have a bus ride. 这也是事实。任何事物都有它的两面性。如果您想体验加拿大的公交车服务,那就走三个街区乘坐一下吧。

A：Good idea. Thank you. 好主意！谢谢。

2. Words and Expressions　单词和词组

(1) citizen　/ˈsɪtɪz(ə)n/　*n.*　公民,市民,老百姓

(2) population　/pɒpjʊˈleɪʃ(ə)n/　*n.*　人口

(3) pack　/pæk/　*v.*　挤,包装；　*n.*　包装,背包

(4) passenger　/ˈpæsɪndʒə/　*n.*　乘客

（5）sardine　/sɑːˈdiːn/　*n*.　沙丁鱼,庸碌无能的人

（6）public transportation　公共交通

（7）only a few　很少,只有几个

（8）since　/sɪns/　*conj*.　既然,由于,自从……以来

（9）fare　/feə/　*n*.　票价,费用

（10）experience　/ɪkˈspɪərɪəns/　*v*.　体验,经历;　*n*.　经验,经历

3. Tips and Notes　要点解释

（1）Taking buses is very convenient.　乘坐公交车非常方便。

这是动名词作主语的句型,注意动名词作主语时作为一个整体,视为单数。如:Having a cup of coffee with friends is really relaxing。和朋友们喝杯咖啡真的很惬意。

（2）when going out　外出时

这是一个用现在分词代替状语从句的句型,原句是"when they go out"。英语中当主句的主语与从句的主语一致时,可以用现在分词作状语。如:You should be careful while crossing the road. 过马路时,您应该小心些。

（3）Each coin has two sides.　任何事物都有它的两面性。

这是英语中的一个常用表达,直译为"每个硬币都有两面",意译为"任何事物都有它的两面性"。

4. Drills　句型操练

（1）Can you tell me ...?

Can you tell me how to get to the park?

Can you tell me what to do with the smart phone?

Can you tell me where to take a bus?

(2) How long will it take to ...?

How long will it take to water the flowers?

How long will it take to get used to the climate here?

How long will it take to walk to the nearest bus stop?

(3) It's very common for sb. to ...

It's very common for people to keep a pet.

It's very common for the seniors to get up early.

It's very common for the young to stay up very late.

5. Recitation　常用句背诵

(1) It's a bit far from here.　它离这里有点远。

(2) Each coin has two sides.　任何事物都有它的两面性。

6. Follow Up　拓展学习

Taking a Bus　乘坐公交车

A＝Visitor 参观者；B＝Bus Driver 公交车司机

A：Excuse me. Does this bus go to the National Library?　打扰一下，这辆车去国家图书馆吗?

B：No. You'll have to get off at the bank，and take Bus No.653.　不到。您得在银行那站下车，然后换乘 653 路公交车。

A：Thank you. How much is the fare to that stop?　谢谢。到那站车票多少钱?

B：One dollar.　1 美元。

A：How many stops?　有几站?

B：Three stops after this one. 这站以后还有三站。

A：By the way, do I need to transfer again after No. 653? 顺便问一下，我从653路下车后还需要再换乘吗？

B：No，not necessary. No. 653 will take you right there. 不需要了，653路公交车直接到那儿。

A：Thank you. 谢谢。

Ⅱ. Community Shuttles in Different Countries
不同国家的社区公交

1. Dialogues 对话

A＝Deniel 丹尼尔；B＝John 约翰

A：Hi，John. Glad to see you here. 嗨，约翰。很高兴在这儿看到您。

B：Hello，Deniel. How is everything? Have you got used to the life here? 您好，丹尼尔。您近况如何？您有没有习惯这里的生活啊？

A：To tell you the truth, I don't like the life here at all. It's about 2 months since I came here. I seldom go out because the bus transportation is not very convenient. You know，I can't drive. 告诉您实话，我一点都不喜欢这里的生活。我来这里大约两个月了，但是我很少出门，因为这里的公共交通不太方便。您知道，我不会开车。

B：Don't worry. I heard in some big cities in Canada, community shuttles have come into service. 别担心。我听说在加拿大的一些大城市已经有社区公交了。

A：Are there any differences between buses and community

shuttles?   公交车和社区公交有什么区别吗?

B：Yes. Community shuttle service is only provided by big communities or universities. And their routes are usually short.   有的。社区公交仅仅是为大型社区或者大学提供的服务,车程很短。

A：I wonder if people can take the community shuttles for free.   不知道人们是否可以免费乘坐社区公交。

B：It depends. Some are free，but some are only free for seniors and the disabled.   这得看情况。有些社区公交是免费的,有些只对老人和残疾人免费。

A：Wow，it seems that the seniors have a lot of privileges.   哇,看起来老年人享有很多特权啊!

B：And all the shuttles are wheelchair accessible.   这类公交车都适用于轮椅使用者。

A：I think it's a thoughtful design.   我认为这种设计考虑得很周到。

B：I'm sure you will get used to the life here soon. Don't stay at home，go out and take part in more community activities.   我相信您很快就会适应这里的生活。别只待在家里,出来走走,多参加一些社区活动。

A：Thank you for your good suggestion.   谢谢您的好建议。

2. Words and Expressions 单词和词组

(1) community /kəˈmjuːnətɪ/ *n.* 社区

(2) shuttle /ˈʃʌt(ə)l/ *n.* 公共汽车,穿梭班机; *v.* 穿梭往返

(3) get used to   习惯

（4）to tell you the truth　说实话,说真话

（5）not ... at all　一点儿也不

（6）seldom　/'seldəm/　*adv.*　很少,不常

（7）come into service　投入使用

（8）disabled　/dɪs'eɪbld/　*adj.*　残疾的,有缺陷的

（9）wheelchair　/'wiːltʃeə/　*n.*　轮椅

（10）accessible　/ək'sesɪb(ə)l/　*adj.*　可进入的,可到达的

（11）thoughtful　/'θɔːtf(ə)l/　*adj.*　体贴的,考虑周到的

3. Tips and Notes　要点解释

（1）get used to（doing）sth.　习惯于（做）某事

与之类似的短语是 be used to（doing）sth。区别是 get used to ...表达渐渐习惯,强调的是从不习惯到习惯的这个过程；be used to ...表达习惯于……,强调的是习惯了……这个状态。如：The food here is not so tasty but you will get used to that.　这里的伙食不怎么样,但您会慢慢习惯的。

（2）It's about 2 months since I came here.　我来这里大约两个月了。

这里的主句主语 it 表示时间,主句的时态用一般现在时代替现在完成时。原句应该为 It has been about 2 months since I came here.

4. Drills　句型操练

（1）Have you got used to ...

Have you got used to the climate here?

Have you got used to living in the countryside?

Have you got used to eating with knife and fork?

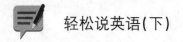

(2) To tell you the truth ...

To tell you the truth, I don't like the local food at all.

To tell you the truth, I often stay up very late at weekends.

To tell you the truth, I have never been in a place for so long.

(3) I wonder if ...

I wonder if I can use your bicycle.

I wonder if he can pass the driving test.

I wonder if you can lend me your bicycle.

5. Recitation　常用句背诵

(1) How is everything?　您近况如何？

(2) It depends.　这得看情况。

(3) Thank you for your good suggestion.　谢谢您的好建议。

6. Follow Up　拓展学习

Bus Cultures in America

In America, all buses are self-service, and bus fares range from 50 cents to 2.5 dollars, which depends on the distance and rush hour. Passengers need to carry exact cash or coins because no change will be given back. All tickets have time limit and can be used for unlimited travel within two hours.

Buses don't stop for all stops and passengers need to press the bell to remind the driver to stop the bus. Taking a bus in America is a pleasant experience, for the driver is friendly and most passengers greet the driver when loading or unloading the bus. In front of the bus there is a metal rack on which bicycles can be placed and fixed. The buses are also designed for the convenience of the seniors and the disabled. There is a lifting plate at the gate of the bus. When those who need help are ready to get on the bus, the lifting plate will be lowered to the ground level for the wheel-chairs to glide on.

美国的公交车文化

美国的公交车都是无人售票的，一张车票在 50 美分到 2.5 美元不等，主要根据距离和是否在上下班高峰时段而定。如果是上车买票，车费不找零钱。车票上面印有买票的时间和失效的时间，一般一张票可用于两个小时内的随意换乘。

美国的公交车不是站站停，也不是每站都报站名，乘客需要提前按一下车上的响铃通知司机自己在下一站下车。在美国乘坐公交车很人性化，司机很热情，大多数乘客上车的时候会和司机打招呼，下车的时候会和司机说谢谢。美国的公交车前面有一个可收放的金属架子，有自行车的乘客，可以在上车前把自行车放在架子上并固定好。美国的公交车也设计得便于老人和残疾人上车。在公交车的车门处有一个液压升降装置，遇到行动不便的老人或坐轮椅的残疾人上公交车的情况，司机会把升降板降到地面，等老人或残疾人的轮椅上到升降板上后，再把板子升起来。

Ⅲ. Schedules of Community Shuttles　社区公交时间表

1. Dialogues　对话

A＝Visitor　参观者；B＝Local Citizen　当地居民

A：Excuse me. Is this the stop of the community shuttle?　打扰一下，这是社区公交的停靠点吗？

B：Yes. Where would you like to go? 是的，您想去哪里？

A：I'd like to go to the Central Park. How often does the community shuttle run? 我想去中央公园。社区公交多长时间一班？

B：About every 30 minutes. 大概每 30 分钟一班。

A：I see. How soon will the next shuttle come? 我明白了。那下一班公交车什么时候到？

B：Let me check the schedule. The next shuttle with stop at the Central Park arrives here at 11：00 a.m. Now it is 10：05 a.m., I feel sorry to say you have to wait for nearly one hour. 我来看一看时间表。停靠中央公园站的下一班车预计在早上 11：00 到达。现在是早上 10：05，您还需要等大约一个小时。

A：One hour? But you said the community shuttle comes every 30 minutes. 一个小时？您刚才不是说社区公交每 30 分钟一班吗？

B：That's right. But the shuttle does not stop at every stop on every run, which means you'd better refer to the schedule to ensure choosing the correct route. 没错。但社区公交每次运行并不会在每个站点都停靠，这意味着您最好参考时间表以确保您选择了正确的路线。

A：Oh, it is quite confusing. The community shuttle is not as convenient as I thought of. Are they free for seniors? 哦，这让我都糊涂了。社区公交没我想的那么方便。老年人可以免费乘坐吗？

B：No，not exactly. They are free for seniors only on Mondays. 不完全免费。社区公交只在周一对老年人免费。

A：Oh, my God! I can't believe my ears. 噢，天哪！我简直不敢相信自己的耳朵。

2. Words and Expressions　单词和词组

(1) schedule　/ˈʃedjuːl/　*n*.　时间表,日程表

(2) run　/rʌn/　*v*.　运行,经营,跑步

(3) every 30 minutes　每 30 分钟

(4) on every run　每一趟运行

(5) refer to　参考

(6) ensure　/ɪnˈʃʊə/　*v*.　确保,保证

(7) confusing　/kənˈfjuːzɪŋ/　*adj*.　令人困惑的,混淆的

3. Tips and Notes　要点解释

(1) how often 是对频率(once a week、three times a month 等)的提问,表达间隔多久;how soon 是对将来一段时间(in an hour、in two weeks 等)的提问,表达再过多久;容易混淆的还有 how long,这是对一段时间(three hours、four years 等)的提问,表达多长时间、多久。

(2) The next shuttle with stop at the Central Park arrives here at 11:00 a.m.　停靠中央公园站的下一班车预计在早上 11:00 到达。

表达按规定、时间表、计划或安排要发生的动作时,可用一般现在时来表达将来的动作。如:The train arrives in Nanjing at 10:45 a.m. and leaves at 10:50 a.m.

(3) not as convenient as I thought of　没我想的那么方便

not as ... as 是 as ... as 的否定句,表示没有像……一样或者不及、不如。两个 as 中间用形容词或者副词的原级。如:I am not as tall as he.　我没有他高。She can not run as fast as I.　她跑得没我快。

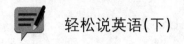

4. Drills　句型操练

（1）How often ...

How often do you walk your dog?

How often does he water the flowers?

How often do you have your car washed?

（2）How soon ...

How soon will he come back?

How soon will you have the dinner ready?

How soon can they move into the new house?

（3）I feel sorry to say ...

I feel sorry to say you have to go there on foot.

I feel sorry to say you have missed the last bus.

I feel sorry to say you have taken the wrong subway.

5. Recitation　常用句背诵

（1）It is quite confusing.　这让我都糊涂了。

（2）I can't believe my ears.　我简直不敢相信自己的耳朵。

6. Follow Up　拓展学习

A Senior Citizen Taking a Bus

My husband, Michael, a bus driver, was passing a deserted bus stop when one of his passengers called out that a woman wanted to get on. He pulled up to the curb and opened the doors.

After a minute, Michael saw an elderly woman with a cane crossing the street slowly.

He waited patiently as she made her way to the bus and climbed the steps.

While she was looking in her purse for her bus pass, he began to close the doors. "Wait a minute!" she snapped. "My mother's coming."

老年人乘坐巴士

我丈夫麦克是一名公交车司机。有一次,当他刚要开过一个无人上下车的车站时,其中一位乘客喊有位老妇人要上车。麦克把车停靠在马路边,打开了车门。

过了一分钟,麦克才见到一位老太太拄着拐杖,慢腾腾地过马路朝车子走来。

麦克耐心地等她来到公交车旁并且爬上台阶。

趁老太太打开钱包找公交卡的工夫,麦克欲关门,老妇人阻止道:"等一会儿,我妈妈还在后面呢!"

手机扫码
听单词和对话

Unit 3　Community Activities
社区活动

Ⅰ.Garage Sale　车库售物

1. Dialogues　对话

A＝Neighbour 邻居；B＝Mike 迈克

A：Hi，Mike. I heard you are moving next week. Has everything been settled?　您好,迈克。我听说您下周要搬家了。一切都安排妥当了吗?

B：Not yet. There are some household appliances and old furniture left. They are too heavy and bulky. I don't know how to deal with them.　还没有。有一些家用电器和旧家具剩下来了,它们太重、太大了。我在想如何处理它们。

A：Why don't you sell them?　为什么不把它们给卖了呢?

B：Sell them? Do you mean to sell them in the flea market?　卖掉? 您是指跳蚤市场吗?

A：No. I think you can use your garage or even the garden to sell them. The Americans have the habit of selling their unused goods or even hot new goods when they are moving to their new homes.　不是。我认为您可以利用您的车库或者院子去出售这些商品。美国人有搬家时卖闲置物品甚至是崭新物品的习惯。

B：I heard about it when I was in China. Where do they display their junks? 我在中国时就听说过这个。他们把旧货摆在哪里呢？

A：They usually display all the stuff they want to get rid of in front of the garage or in their yards at the weekend. 他们经常会在周末把要处理的东西摆在车库门前或者院子里。

B：Have you ever been to a garage sale? 您是否参加过车库售物？

A：I didn't have any idea until last month when I came to a big garage sale. Many things people were selling still looked quite new and very useful. 直到上个月我去了一个大型的车库售物，才对它有所了解。里面出售的很多东西都很新，很实用。

B：Did you find anything that attracted you? 您有没有找到吸引您的东西？

A：Yes，I did. The shopping experience there was quite different from that in shopping malls. People can chat with each other，drink coffee or tea and make a bargain. It's very common that you can buy a wonderful article at a throw-away price. 是的。那里的购物体验与购物中心截然不同。人们在一起聊天，喝咖啡或者喝茶，讨价还价。通常，您能以一个相当优惠的价格买到一个很不错的物品。

B：That sounds very good. 听起来真不错。

2. Words and Expressions 单词和词组

（1）garage /ˈɡærɑːʒ/ n. 车库，汽车修理厂

（2）settle /ˈsetl/ v. 安排，解决，定居

（3）household /ˈhaʊshəʊld/ n. 家庭；adj. 家用的

27

(4) appliance /ə'plaɪəns/ *n.* 家用电器

(5) household appliances 家用电器

(6) furniture /'fɜːnɪtʃə(r)/ *n.* 家具

(7) bulky /'bʌlkɪ/ *adj.* 庞大的,笨重的

(8) deal with 处理,做生意

(9) flea /fliː/ *n.* 跳蚤

(10) have the habit of 有……的习惯

(11) unused /ˌʌn'juːzd/ *adj.* 不用的,从未用过的

(12) hear about 听说

(13) stuff /stʌf/ *n.* 东西,填充物; *v.* 塞满,填塞

(14) get rid of 摆脱,除去

(15) yard /jɑːd/ *n.* 院子,庭院,码

(16) bargain /'bɑːgən/ *n.* 便宜货; *v.* 讨价还价

(17) make a bargain 讨价还价,成交

(18) at a throw-away price 以抛售价

3. Tips and Notes 要点解释

(1) I heard you are moving next week. 我听说您下周要搬家了。

在这里,are moving 表示将要发生的动作。英语中表示位置移动的一些动词(如 come、go、leave、move、fly 等)可用进行时表示将要发生的动作。如:My friend Lily is coming to see me next month. 我的朋友 Lily 将在下个月来看我。

(2) I didn't have any idea until last month... 直到上个月我……才对它有所了解。

这句话中使用了 not ... until 的句型,翻译为"直到……才"。

如：I didn't understand this problem until my teacher explained it to me. 直到老师给我解释后，我才理解这道题目。

（3）The shopping experience there was quite different from that in shopping malls.　那里的购物体验与购物中心截然不同。

这句话中的 that 用以替代前面的 the shopping experience。在英语比较句中，为了避免重复，经常用 that、those 等词来替代前面提到过的名词。that 替代单数名词，those 替代复数名词。如：The weather here is warmer than that in Shanghai.　这里的天气比上海的天气热。

4. Drills　句型操练

（1）Why don't you ...?

Why don't you join us?

Why don't you try a garage sale?

Why don't you go to the flea market?

（2）I think you can ...

I think you can have a try.

I think you can make a bargain with them.

I think you can find something useful in the flea market.

（3）contact

Keep in contact.

She's lost contact with her son for three months.

Have you been able to have any kind of contact?

5. Recitation　常用句背诵

（1）Has everything been settled?　一切都安排妥当了吗?

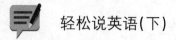

（2）Have you ever been to a garage sale?　您是否参加过车库售物？

（3）Wish you good luck.　祝您好运。

6. Follow Up　拓展学习

Yard Sale

Yard sale，also called garage sale，is a very special way of selling in America. The sellers put all the stuff they want to get rid of outside their houses，e.g. the yard，garage or porch. There will always be some advertisements which tell what stuff will be for sale as well as when and where the yard sale will take place. The price of each item is also written in the tag. There are a wide variety of stuffs，most of which are used and some are even hot new. To attract more buyers，yard sale often takes place at weekends.

One person's useless，ugly，or broken object can be another person's treasure. Many Americans like going to yard sale，hoping to find something special. Yard sale is very popular especially in autumn. For some reasons，Americans often move. They don't want to bother themselves with carrying tons of luggage，as a result，yard sale appears. They put all the junks outside and put on a "For Sale" sign.

庭院售物

庭院售物又称车库售物,是美国一种独特的售物方式。主人把家中不用的物品放在庭院中、车库里或门廊下廉价出售。主人会在手写的广告中详细列出售卖的东西、时间和地点,还会用标签注明每件物品的价格。被廉价处理的物品多种多样,多数是用过的东西,但也有全新的物品。为了吸引更多买主,这种售物活动常在周末举行。

很多美国人喜欢周末逛旧货摊,希望能够"人弃我取",在别人不要的东西里找到自己的宝贝。在秋高气爽的季节,庭院售物特别活跃。由于种种原因,美国人搬家频繁,为免除大包小包的麻烦,庭院售物就格外多。他们把那些东西拿到门外,然后插上一个"出售"的牌子,庭院售物就开始了。

Ⅱ. Community Center　社区中心

1. Dialogues　对话

A＝Service Staff 服务人员；B＝Elder 长者

A：Good morning, customer service. What can I do for you?　早上好,这里是客户服务部。我能为您做点什么吗?

B：I was told that a wide range of courses are offered in your community center. And I wonder if there are any programs for seniors.　有人告诉我你们的社区中心提供很多课程,我不知道有没有给老年人提供的课程。

A：We have different programs for all ages, ranging from the kindergarten kids to seniors. As for adults aged over 50, we have five senior citizen centers. Here is the guide and you can see page ten for their location map.　我们的课程涵盖各个年龄段,从上幼儿园的孩子到老年人。对于 50 岁以上的人,我们有五个中心。这是手册,您可以在第十页查看它们的地图方位。

B：Thank you. Would you be kind enough to introduce some courses to me briefly?　谢谢。您能给我简短介绍一下课程吗?

A：My pleasure. There are a great number of programs for seniors, such as dancing, watercolour painting, knitting, guitar playing, fitness keeping, playing Tai Ji and so on. You can make a choice. 没问题。针对老年人开设的课程有很多，如跳舞、画水彩画、编织、弹吉他、健身、打太极等。您可以自己选择。

B：I have learnt watercolour painting for two years in China. Do I have to start from the very beginning? 我在中国学过两年的水彩画，那我还需要从头开始学吗？

A：No, you don't. There are different levels for seniors to choose. Since you have learnt watercolour painting for two years, Level 2 will be more suitable for you. It's up to you. 不用。有不同的级别可以供老年人选择。既然您已经学过两年的水彩画，二级班更适合您。您自行决定。

B：Thank you. I think Level 2 is suitable for me. By the way, I want to take a course of fitness keeping. Can you recommend some? 谢谢。我认为二级班更适合我。顺便问一下，我还想健身锻炼，您能推荐一下吗？

A：There are a wide range of selections. Cycling, drum fitness, hall walking, and Tai Ji, to name a few. You can make a choice according to your physical conditions. 有很多选择，如骑自行车、鼓点健身、大厅行走、打太极等。您可以根据自己的身体情况选择。

B：Can I have any drop-in programs? 有不用预约的课程吗？

A：Yes. The community centers offer a variety of drop-in programs, workshops, travel and volunteer opportunities for various interests and abilities at different levels. 有的。社区中心给不同兴趣和能力的会员提供了各种各样的不用预约的课程、讲习

班、旅行以及当志愿者的机会。

　　B：That's exactly what I want.　这正是我想要的。

2. Words and Expressions　单词和词组

（1）range　/reɪndʒ/　v.　（在……内）变动；　n.　范围，幅度

（2）a wide range of　各种各样的，大范围的

（3）kindergarten　/ˈkɪndəɡɑːtn/　n.　幼儿园

（4）as for　关于，至于

（5）a great number of　大量的

（6）watercolour　/ˈwɔːtərkʌlə/　n.　水彩画；　adj.　水彩的

（7）knit　/nɪt/　v.　编织，针织

（8）fitness keeping　健身

（9）Tai Ji　太极

（10）make a choice　做出选择

（11）from the very beginning　从头开始，从一开始

（12）up to sb.　由某人选择，自行决定

（13）selection　/sɪˈlekʃn/　n.　选择，挑选

（14）to name a few　举几个例子来说

（15）drop-in　/ˈdrɒp ɪn/　adj.　不用预约的，立即使用的

（16）a variety of　各种各样的

3. Tips and Notes　要点解释

　　（1）Would you be kind enough to introduce some courses to me briefly?　您能给我简短介绍一下课程吗?

　　这里的 enough 表示"足够"，应放在形容词、副词或动词的后面，放在名词的前面。如：He is strong enough to lift the stone.　他足

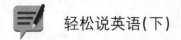

够强壮去举起这块石头。　I don't have enough time to keep fit. 我没有足够的时间去健身。

（2）from the very beginning　从头开始，从一开始

这里的 very 表示强调。如：He is the very person you're looking for.　他就是您要找的那个人。

4. Drills　句型操练

（1）Would you be kind enough to …?

Would you be kind enough to look after my dog?

Would you be kind enough to pick me up at the airport?

Would you be kind enough to give me a lift to the community center?

（2）Do I have to …?

Do I have to wait for you here?

Do I have to finish the work today?

Do I have to renew my membership card in this center?

（3）There be … for … to …

There are different courses for you to choose.

There are many places of interest for me to visit.

There is much room for Chinese buses to get improved.

5. Recitation　常用句背诵

（1）It's up to you.　您自行决定。

（2）That's exactly what I want.　这正是我想要的。

6. Follow Up   拓展学习

Welcome to our community center! We have different clubs. It is a great place to keep fit and enjoy yourselves!   欢迎来到社区中心！我们有各种各样的俱乐部，是保持健康、愉悦身心的好地方！

Ball Games Club You can play volleyball, tennis or other ball games here.		3:00 p.m. ~ 10:00 p.m. Tel: 3754789
Swimming Club It's really cool!		6:00 a.m. ~ 10:00 p.m. Tel: 3754753
Free Classes No need to pay any money.	Dancing	8:00 a.m. ~ 11:00 a.m. Tel: 3754676
	Roller skating	1:00 p.m. ~ 6:00 p.m. Tel: 375 - 762
Kids Club We have drawing, dancing, swimming classes for kids aged 3 to 6. They can play games and make friends here.		8:00 a.m. ~ 6:00 p.m. Tel: 375 - 766

译文如下：

球类俱乐部 这里可以打排球、网球或者开展其他球类运动。		下午 3:00 ~ 晚上 10:00 电话：3754789
游泳俱乐部 超级酷！		上午 6:00 ~ 晚上 10:00 电话：3754753
免费课程 无须付费。	舞蹈	上午 8:00 ~ 上午 11:00 电话：3754676
	溜冰	下午 1:00 ~ 下午 6:00 电话：375 - 762
儿童俱乐部 针对 3 至 6 岁的儿童，我们提供绘画、跳舞、游泳课程，孩子们可以在这里玩游戏、交朋友。		上午 8:00 ~ 下午 6:00 电话：375 - 766

Ⅲ. To Be Invited for Dinner　应邀做客

1. Dialogues　对话

A＝Visitor 参观者；B＝Sarah 莎拉

A：Hi，Sarah，can you do me a favor?　嗨，莎拉。您能帮我一个忙吗?

B：Sure. What happened?　当然可以。怎么啦?

A：My neighbour，Mrs. Johnson，invited me to have dinner in her house this weekend. I'm not sure what gifts to take on the first visit. Can you give me some suggestions?　我的邻居约翰逊太太邀请我这个周末到她家里吃饭。我不确定第一次拜访带什么礼物合适，您能给我一些建议吗?

B：No problem. How to bring gifts is a kind of art.　没问题。如何赠送礼物是一门艺术。

A：Yes. What about that in America?　是的。送礼文化在美国是怎样的呢?

B：Gift giving is not as important in America as it is in other countries. So there is nothing wrong not to give a gift in America. But you can choose to bring a small gift.　在美国，送礼物不像在其他国家那样重要。因此，在美国不送礼物也没什么错。但是您可以选择送一个小礼物。

A：A bottle of wine，cosmetics，cut flowers or something else?　一瓶酒、化妆品、鲜花，还是其他什么呢?

B：Don't bring too valuable gifts on the first visit. For men，don't give anything of a personal nature，such as cosmetics， perfume or clothes，to a woman. A scarf would be more suitable for this occasion.　第一次拜访不要送太贵重的礼物，对男士来说，不要送私人性质的东西给女性，如化妆品、香水、服装等，在这种场合送围巾更合适些。

A：That's a good suggestion. Thank you very much.　这个建议太好了。非常感谢。

2. Words and Expressions　单词和词组

（1）be invited for dinner　受邀做客

（2）do sb. a favor　帮某人一个忙

（3）invite sb. to have dinner　邀请某人吃饭

（4）on the first visit　第一次拜访

（5）cosmetic　/kɒz'metɪk/　*n*．化妆品

（6）valuable　/'væljuəbl/　*adj*．贵重的，有价值的

（7）nature　/'neɪtʃə(r)/　*n*．性质，自然

（8）of a personal nature　私人性质的

（9）perfume　/'pɜːfjuːm/　*n*．香水，香味

（10）scarf　/skɑːf/　*n*．围巾，头巾

（11）occasion　/ə'keɪʒn/　*n*．场合，时机

3. Tips and Notes　要点解释

（1）How to bring gifts is a kind of art.　如何赠送礼物是一门艺术。

这里 How to 引导的动词不定式作句子的主语。英语句子结构中，疑问词＋to do 可以在句中作主语、宾语、表语等。如：What to do next is still not decided.　下一步做什么还没有决定。The

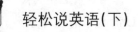
problem is when to do this task.　问题是何时执行这个任务。

(2) Don't give anything of a personal nature.　不要送私人性质的东西。

这个句子中 of＋...名词的结构,相当于一个形容词。如：I want to buy some books of great value.　我想买些有价值的书。The bike is of no use.　这辆自行车没有用了。

4. Drills　句型操练

(1) I'm not sure ...

I'm not sure what to do next.

I'm not sure where to have my computer repaired.

I'm not sure whether to buy a new computer or not.

(2) ... is considered (to be) ...

He is considered (to be) very honest.

Talking loudly in public is considered (to be) rude.

Shaking hands with others is considered (to be) good manners.

(3) I happened to ...

I happened to have that book.

I happened to be on a trip this Sunday.

I happened to know her telephone number.

5. Recitation　常用句背诵

(1) Can you do me a favor?　您能帮我一个忙吗?

(2) What happened?　怎么啦?

(3) Can you give me some suggestions?　您能给我一些建议吗?

6. Follow Up 拓展学习

Different Customs in Different Countries of Giving Presents

In Germany, flowers are a good present to give to the hostess, but don't take her red roses because it means you are in love with her. Don't wrap your present in white, brown, or black paper or ribbon. What's more, never give something sharp.

In Britain, give gifts not expensive but meaningful, such as chocolates of supreme quality, fine wine, flowers and so on. Lilies are not appropriate for gifts. It's a custom for the receivers to open the wrapped gifts in public.

In America, practical or peculiar gifts are welcome, especially small gifts with distinctive national features. Good packing is important, but don't wrap your present in black paper. Give gifts with odd numbers. Remember not to give perfume, cosmetics or clothes (excluding headscarf) to ladies as a gift.

In Japan, don't open the gift in public. Remember to mention the gift and express your gratitude when seeing again the person who gives the gift. Combs, gifts with fox or badger pictures and chrysanthemum should be avoided as a gift.

In the Netherlands, don't give expensive gifts. Gifts need to be beautifully wrapped. If you are invited to a Dutch home, bring a bunch of flowers, a box of chocolates or a bottle of wine. Remember not to be too agreeable to the hostess.

In Russia, if you give flowers as a gift, you have to give odd numbers of them . Never give money to others as a gift, because it means alms and insult.

不同国家赠送礼物的习俗

德国:送礼讲究包装,忌送玫瑰花。礼品切勿用白色、棕色、黑色的包装纸或丝带包扎。另外,不要送尖锐的器物。

英国:一般送价格不贵但有纪念意义的礼物,如高品质的巧克力、名酒和鲜花等。忌送百合。收到礼物的人应当众打开礼物。

美国:美国人对礼品主要讲究实用性和奇特性。如果能送一些具有独特风格或民族特色的小礼品,美国人会很欢迎。包装礼品时不要用黑色的纸,送礼物要送单数,且讲究包装。忌给女性送香水、化妆品和衣物(可送头巾)。

日本:不能当面打开礼物。再次见到送礼的人时要提及礼物的事,并表示感谢。忌送梳子,也不要送有狐狸、獾图案的礼物,一般情况下也不能送菊花。

荷兰:送礼忌送贵重物品,且礼物要包装精美。到荷兰人家里做客,可以带上一束鲜花或者是巧克力、葡萄酒等,切勿对女主人过于殷勤。

俄罗斯:送鲜花要送单数,最忌讳送钱给他人,这意味着施舍与侮辱。

Unit 4   Seeing a Doctor
看病就诊

Ⅰ. In the Emergency Center   急诊中心

1. Dialogues   对话

A＝Helen 海伦；B＝Peter 彼得；C＝Emergency Center Receptionist 急诊中心接待员

（At Home   在家中）

A：Hello, Peter. This is Helen. Ten minutes ago, I missed a step and slid onto the floor when I was watering my flowers. Unluckily, it seems that my right ankle is twisted. I can't stand now. Would you please send me to the nearest Emergency Center?   嗨，彼得。我是海伦。10分钟前我浇花的时候踩空一步，滑倒了。不幸的是，我的右脚好像扭伤了，我站不起来，您能把我送到最近的急诊中心吗？

B：No problem. Stay at home and I will be there soon.   没问题。你待在家里，我很快就到。

（At the Emergency Center   在急诊中心）

C：Good morning. Please fill out the information on this form.   早上好，请在这张表上填好信息。

A：My right ankle is probably twisted. I want to see a surgeon.   我的右脚好像扭伤了，我要挂外科。

C：Do you have medical insurance?   您有医疗保险吗？

A：Yes，I do.   我有医疗保险。

41

C：Please let me see your medical card. OK，now first let me take your temperature ... and then your blood pressure ... Uh, your blood pressure is a little bit too high.　请把医保卡给我看一下。好的，我先给您量一下体温……再测一下您的血压……哦，您的血压有点高。

A：Can you tell me the exact reading?　您能告诉我具体血压吗？

C：Um，the systolic pressure is 190，and the diastolic pressure is 100. Are you on any blood pressure medications recently?　嗯，收缩压 190，舒张压 100。您最近在吃降压药吗？

A：Yes，I have taken the blood pressure medications for about 10 years.　对的，我吃降压药大约已经 10 年了。

C：What's your blood type?　您的血型是什么？

A：Type B.　B 型。

C：Are you allergic to any medications?　您对药物过敏吗？

A：I'm not sure.　我不太确定。

C：OK. Put this ice bag on your injured ankle and don't move. It will help you feel better. The doctor will come to examine you in a few minutes.　好的。请用这个冰袋敷着您的受伤处，不要移动。这会让您好受一些。医生一会儿会来检查。

A：Thank you.　谢谢。

2. Words and Expressions　单词和词组

（1）emergency　/ɪˈmɜːdʒənsɪ/　n.　急诊病人，急诊室

（2）Emergency Center　急诊中心

（3）miss a step　踩空一步

（4）ankle　/ˈæŋk(ə)l/　n.　踝关节，脚踝

（5）twist　/twɪst/　v. & n.　扭伤，扭曲

（6）fill out　填写

（7）surgeon　/ˈsɜːdʒ(ə)n/　n.　外科医生

（8）medical insurance　医疗保险

（9）blood pressure　血压

（10）systolic /sɪ'stɒlɪk/　*adj.*　心脏收缩的

（11）systolic pressure　收缩压

（12）diastolic /ˌdaɪə'stɒlɪk/　*adj.*　心脏舒张的

（13）diastolic pressure　舒张压

（14）medication /medɪ'keɪʃ(ə)n/　*n.*　药物,药物治疗

（15）blood pressure medications　降压药

（16）blood type　血型

（17）allergic /ə'lɜːdʒɪk/　*adj.*　对……过敏的

（18）be allergic to …　对……过敏

（19）injured /'ɪndʒəd/　*adj.*　受伤的,受损害的

3. Tips and Notes　要点解释

（1）a little bit 意思是一点点,与 a bit 相同,后面可以修饰形容词或者副词。如：I am a little bit tired now.　我现在有点累。She speaks a little bit fast.　她说话有点快。

（2）medicine 是普通用词,可指药物的总称。如：You need to take some medicine.　您需要吃药。medication 尤指医院用于治疗病人的药。如：He is on medication now.　他正在接受药物治疗。

4. Drills　句型操练

（1）Would you please …?

Would you please open the window?

Would you please pass the salt to me?

Would you please ask him to call me back?

（2）Stay at home and I will …（祈使句＋and/or＋陈述句将来时）

Stay there and I will come to find you.

Go out for a walk and you will feel better.

Join the Senior Clubs and you will make more friends.

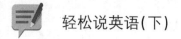
(3) I learn that …

I learn that he is ill.

I learn that she has a son and a daughter.

I learn that we'll visit Shanghai Disneyland next week.

5. Recitation　常用句背诵

(1) Are you allergic to any medications?　您对药物过敏吗?

(2) I'm sorry to hear that.　听说这件事, 我很抱歉。

6. Follow Up　拓展学习

Doctor ! I Need Your Help!

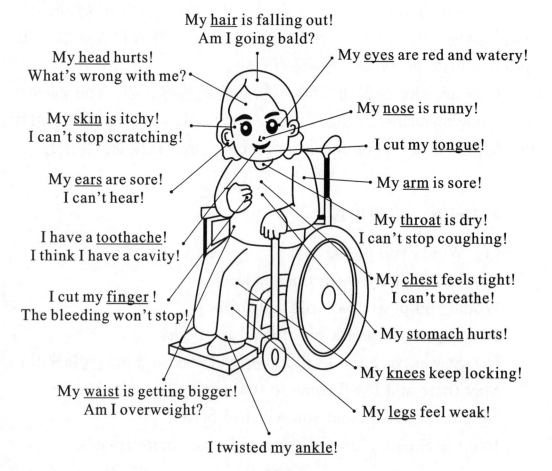

My hair is falling out!
Am I going bald?

My head hurts!
What's wrong with me?

My eyes are red and watery!

My skin is itchy!
I can't stop scratching!

My nose is runny!

I cut my tongue!

My ears are sore!
I can't hear!

My arm is sore!

My throat is dry!
I can't stop coughing!

I have a toothache!
I think I have a cavity!

My chest feels tight!
I can't breathe!

I cut my finger !
The bleeding won't stop!

My stomach hurts!

My knees keep locking!

My waist is getting bigger!
Am I overweight?

My legs feel weak!

I twisted my ankle!

Ⅱ. Have an Examination 医院检查

1. Dialogues 对话

A＝Helen 海伦；B＝Peter 彼得；C＝Doctor 医生

A：Oh, my God! It seems as if I have waited for a century. 哦,天啊! 感觉我等了一个世纪了。

B：Take it easy. 别着急。

C：Hi, I'm Dr. Smith. So your right ankle hurts? 嗨,我是史密斯医生。您是右脚疼吗?

A：Yes, doctor. It really hurts and it's swelled. 没错,而且真的很疼,已经肿起来了。

C：You need to get it X-rayed to help me judge if it's only a sprain. 您需要拍一个 X 光片,以便于我判断是否只是扭伤。

A：If it's a bone fracture, do I need to be operated on? 如果是骨折,我需要动手术吗?

C：It depends. Now just have your right ankle X-rayed before I make out a diagnosis. 这得看情况。在我得出诊断结果前,您还是先去拍一个 X 光片吧。

（Moments Later 一段时间后）

C：The X-ray picture shows that there's nothing serious. Your ankle is not broken but your ankle ligament is slightly torn. 从 X 光片上看,没什么严重问题。您没有骨折,但是您的脚踝韧带轻微撕裂了。

A：Bad luck. What should I do? 真糟糕! 我该怎么做呢?

C：In my opinion, you had better wear a cast. It will help your ankle ligament recover faster. 我认为您最好绑上石膏,这有助于您的脚踝韧带更快恢复。

A：Wear a cast? But it will be inconvenient for me. Are there any other ways? 绑石膏?这对我来说太不方便了。还有其他办法吗?

C：Hum, you can try the physiotherapy. 嗯,您可以试一试物理疗法。

A：Physiotherapy? 物理疗法?

C：Yes. First, use the ice bag on the injured part for 20 to 30 minutes every 2 to 3 hours. 24 hours later, you can use a hot pack to ease the pain. 是的。首先,每2至3个小时用冰袋敷在受伤处20至30分钟。24小时后,您可以通过热敷来减轻痛感。

A：OK, is that all? 好的,就这些吗?

C：No. Second, have a good rest for 2 to 3 weeks with your right leg raised higher above the level of your heart. Last but not the least, secure with an elastic bandage. 不。其次,好好休息2至3周,并把受伤的脚踝抬高至心脏水平线之上,这对缓解肿胀有好处。最后一点但同样重要的是,用弹性绷带固定。

A：I got it. Thank you very much, doctor. 我明白了。谢谢您,医生。

2. Words and Expressions 单词和词组

（1）examination /ɪɡˌzæmɪˈneɪʃən/ n. 检查

（2）century /ˈsentʃərɪ/ n. 世纪,百年

（3）take it easy 从容,别着急

（4）swell　/swel/　v. & n.　肿胀，隆起

（5）X-ray　/'eks,reɪ/　v.　用 X 光线检查；　n.　射线，射线照片

（6）sprain　/spreɪn/　n. & v.　扭伤

（7）fracture　/'fræktʃə/　n.　外科，骨折，断裂

（8）operate　/'ɒpəreɪt/　v.　做手术

（9）it depends　这得看情况

（10）diagnosis　/,daɪəg'nəʊsɪs/　n.　诊断

（11）ligament　/'lɪgəm(ə)nt/　n.　韧带，纽带

（12）tear　/teə(r)/　v.　撕裂，撕扯；　n.　眼泪

（13）opinion　/ə'pɪnjən/　n.　意见，主张

（14）in my opinion　依我来看，我认为

（15）cast　/kɑːst/　n.　模子，铸件，（固定断骨用）石膏

（16）wear a cast　绑石膏

（17）recover　/rɪ'kʌvə/　v.　恢复

（18）inconvenient　/ɪnkən'viːnɪənt/　adj.　不便的

（19）physiotherapy　/,fɪzɪə(ʊ)'θerəpɪ/　n.　物理疗法

（20）hot pack　热敷

（21）ease　/iːz/　v.　减轻，缓和；　n.　轻松，舒适，安逸

（22）last but not the least　最后一点但同样重要的是

（23）secure　/sɪ'kjʊə; sɪ'kjɔː/　v.　缚住，保护；　adj.　安全的，有把握的

（24）elastic　/ɪ'læstɪk/　adj.　有弹性的

（25）bandage　/'bændɪdʒ/　n.　绷带

（26）elastic bandage　弹性绷带

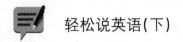

3. Tips and Notes 要点解释

（1）It seems/looks as if … 看起来，好像……

从句的语气要根据句子意思来确定。如果主句表达可能实现的事情，从句用陈述语气；如果主句表达与事实不符的情况，从句用虚拟语气。如：It seems as if it is going to rain. 天看起来要下雨（可能会下雨）。It seems as if she had been to England. 看起来她去过英格兰（事实上，她没去过英格兰）。

（2）You need to get it X-rayed … 您需要拍一个 X 光片……

这里用的是 get sth. done 的结构，英语中 have/get sth. done 表示：使/让……做，或者让他人做某事，强调宾语 sth. 与过去分词之间的被动关系。如：I will have/get my hair cut tomorrow. 我明天去剪头发（让理发师剪）。

（3）Do I need to be operated on? 我需要动手术吗？

这里用的是 need to be done 的结构，强调主语 I 与 operate 之间的被动关系。如：Does the cat need to be fed now? 现在需要喂这只猫吗？

4. Drills 句型操练

（1）It seems as if …

It seems as if he knew everything.

It seems as if our group is going to win.

It seems as if they had known each other for a long time.

（2）Do I need to …?

Do I need to get my ankle X-rayed?

Do I need to be sent to hospital at once?

Do I need to finish the work before dark?

（3）In my opinion，you had better ...

In my opinion，you had better keep a pet.

In my opinion，you had better go to see a doctor.

In my opinion，you had better have your hair cut tomorrow.

5. Recitation　常用句背诵

（1）Take it easy.　别着急。

（2）What should I do?　我该怎么做呢?

（3）Is that all?　就这些吗?

6. Follow Up　拓展学习

How to Go to a Walk-in Clinic

If you have a medical emergency in an English-speaking country, call 112，999 or 911（or the emergency number of the country you are in），or go to a hospital emergency room（ER）. The ER may have a very long wait. If your medical problem is less serious，go to a walk-in clinic. Look online or in a phonebook for the closest clinic. Use the search "walk-in clinic" plus the name of the city you are in. In a phonebook，look under "doctor" or "medical". Check the clinic hours. You don't need an appointment at most clinics. You might want to bring a dictionary or a friend who can translate.

Documents to Bring

If you are a visitor，you will probably be billed for your visit. Bring your papers with you if you have insurance. Bring your prescription form or bottle of medication with you.

如何前往一个免预约诊所

如果您在英语国家/地区遇到医疗紧急情况,请致电 112、999 或 911(或您所在国家/地区的紧急电话号码),或前往医院急诊室 (ER)。ER 可能需要等待很长时间。如果您的情况不太严重,请前往免预约诊所。您可以在线或在电话簿中查找最近的诊所。在线可通过输入"免预约诊所"加上您所在城市的名称进行搜索。在电话簿中,在"医生"或"医疗"词条下进行查找。请您关注诊所的就诊时间,大多数诊所都不需要预约。赴诊时,您也许要带一本字典或一位可以为您翻译的朋友。

需要携带的物品

如果您是游客,您可能需要付费。如果您有保险,请带上您的保险卡,并随身携带处方或药瓶。

Ⅲ. Review and Check Out　复查结账

1. Dialogues　对话

A＝Helen 海伦；B＝Emergency Center Receptionist 急诊中心接待员；C＝Doctor 医生

B：It's your turn, Ms. Helen Xiao. Dr. Smith is waiting for you now in Room 311.　肖海伦女士,轮到您了。史密斯医生在 311 号诊室等您。

C：Hello, Helen. How do you feel now?　您好,海伦。您现在感觉如何?

A：Thank you very much, Dr. Smith. My ankle doesn't hurt at all. I feel much better and I can walk normally now. I needn't take any medicine.　谢谢您,史密斯医生。我的脚踝一点儿也不痛了,我

现在感觉良好,能正常行走了。我不需要服药了。

C：Let me have a look. Uh，it doesn't swell either. It seems that you are well recovered.　让我来看一下。嗯,也消肿了。看起来您恢复得不错。

A：See? I can walk normally now (Walk some steps).　看到了吗？我现在能正常行走了(走了几步)。

C：Good. Now I'm sure your ankle has recovered.　不错。现在我确定您的脚踝已经恢复了。

A：Thank you so much, Dr. Smith.　非常感谢您,史密斯医生。

　　……

A：Excuse me，can I have my bill? My name is Helen Xiao.
打扰一下,我可以看一下账单吗？我是肖海伦。

B：OK. Just wait a moment.　好的。请稍等。

A：Thanks.　谢谢。

B：Sorry for having kept you waiting. It's 7,800 dollars altogether. Because you used the urgent care, the insurance company will only bear a maximum of 60%.　抱歉让您久等了。这是您的账单,一共是 7,800 美元。因为您用的是急诊,保险公司能承担最多 60% 的费用。

A：I can't believe my ears. It's beyond my imagination. Do I need to pay now?　我简直不敢相信我的耳朵,这超出了我的想象。我现在需要付款吗？

B：No，you needn't. We will send the bill to the insurance company first，who will pay about 60% of the bill. Then you will receive the bill from the insurance company and pay the rest of it.　不,您不需要。我们会先把账单寄给保险公司,他们将支付您账单的大约 60%

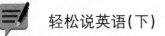

的费用。然后您会收到保险公司寄给您的账单,您只需要支付剩余部分的费用。

A：OK，I see.　好的,我明白了。

B：What else can I do for you?　还有其他需要我做的吗?

A：No，thank you.　没有了,谢谢。

B：My pleasure. Have a good day.　不客气,祝您愉快!

2. Words and Expressions　单词和词组

(1) normally　/'nɔːm(ə)lɪ/　*adv.*　正常地,通常地,一般地

(2) be well recovered　恢复得不错

(3) altogether　/ˌɔːltəˈgeðə(r)/　*adv.*　总共,完全地

(4) insurance company　保险公司

(5) bear　/beə/　*v.*　承担(费用),承受

(6) maximum　/'mæksɪməm/　*n.*　最大量,最大限度；*adj.*　最高的,最多的

(7) beyond one's imagination　超出了……的想象

(8) rest　/rest/　*n.*　剩余部分,休息；*v.*　(使)休息,(使)轻松

3. Tips and Notes　要点解释

(1) I needn't take any medicine.　我不需要服药了。

本句中的 need 为情态动词,也可以写成 I don't need to take any medicine.　下面例句中的 need 为实义动词。如：You needn't see a doctor.　您不需要看病。可以改成 You don't need to see a doctor.

(2) Sorry for having kept you waiting.　抱歉让您久等了。

这是一个省略句,原句是 I'm sorry for having kept you waiting.这

句话可以用在很多场合,如朋友聚会、开车接人、服务员上菜时晚到,都可以用这句话来表达歉意。

4. Drills　句型操练

（1）Let me/him/her/us/them ...

Let him have a try.

Let her open the gift box.

Let us do something for you.

（2）Have a good day.

Have a good trip.

Have a nice weekend.

Wish you happiness and good health forever.

（3）There is no need for you/him/me/us to ...

There is no need for him to explain it again.

There is no need for me to waste time shopping.

There is no need for us to buy so many useless junks.

5. Recitation　常用句背诵

（1）I can't believe my ears.　我简直不敢相信我的耳朵。

（2）It's beyond my imagination.　这超出了我的想象。

（3）Sorry for having kept you waiting.　抱歉让您久等了。

（4）Have a good day.　祝您愉快!

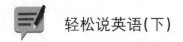

6. Follow Up 拓展学习

About Challenging a Medical Bill

All medical bills are negotiable. If you're thinking of disputing a medical charge, here are some pointers.

Keep good notes. From the very first phone call, write down the date, time and the name of the person to whom you speak.

Request the right bill. If you're questioning hospital charges, you will want to ask for a bill that details every single charge individually.

Start with a phone call. Whatever you do, keep calling until you get the right person on the line. Be both patient and persistent, because you're going to have to go through several levels of challenges.

Follow up in writing. After your initial call, put your request in writing and mail it. Then fax it as well.

Do your research. Start with a site such as HealthcareBluebook.com, which can help you estimate prices for a procedure in your area. Alternatively, some insurers offer a way to price healthcare services.

Don't worry about your quality of care. You shouldn't be concerned that your doctor is going to compromise your quality of care if you challenge a bill.

Get help if you need it. If you're really overwhelmed or facing an enormous amount of medical debt, consider talking to a medical billing advocate, who can help you locate errors in your bills and haggle with healthcare providers on your behalf.

质疑医疗账单

所有医疗费用都可以协商，如果您正在考虑协商医疗费用，请参阅以下内容。

做好记录。从第一个电话开始，记下日期、时间以及对话者的姓名。

要求医院提供正确的账单。如果您对医院的收费有异议，您将需要一份详细记录每项费用的账单。

从打电话开始。无论您做什么，都请持续打电话，直到您找到对接的人。这一过程必须耐心、坚持，因为您将不得不经历一些挑战。

写信跟进。初次通话后，以书面形式提出请求并邮寄。然后再传真。

进行调查研究。使用 HealthcareBluebook.com 等网站，可以帮助您估算您所在地区的手术价格。或者选择部分保险公司为医疗服务定价的方法。

不要担心护理质量。即使您质疑账单，您也不必担心医生会降低对您的护理质量。

如果需要，请寻求帮助。如果您真的不知所措或面临巨额医疗债务，请考虑与医疗账单律师交谈，他们可以帮助您查找账单中的错误并代表您与医疗服务提供者协商。

Unit 5　As a Children's Caregiver
照看儿孙

Ⅰ. Child-care Center　托儿所

1. Dialogues　对话

A＝Neighbour 邻居；B＝Mrs. Zhang 张太太

A：Hello，Mrs. Zhang. You look tired and pale. What's up?　您好，张太太。您看上去很累，脸色也不好。怎么啦？

B：I haven't slept well recently. My grandson Eddie is too energetic and he seldom feels tired. I have to stay up late to play with him. And I can't fall asleep after midnight. As a matter of fact，I have been sleepless for some time.　我最近没睡好觉。我的孙子埃迪精力实在太旺盛了，他很少觉得累，我不得不熬夜陪他，而我过了半夜就睡不着了。事实上，我已经失眠一段时间了。

A：Why not send him to the child-care center? There is a good child-care center in our community，and children between 1 and 4 years can have early learning and care in that center.　为什么不送他去上托儿所呢？我们社区有一家不错的托儿所，1 岁至 4 岁的孩子都可以在那里进行早期学习并接受照顾。

B：Sounds great. Does the center operate from Monday to Friday?　听起来很棒。这家托儿所周一至周五都开放的吧？

A：Yes，it operates Monday to Friday from 7：00 a.m. till 6：00 p.m.，year-round.　是的,全年的周一至周五,早上 7 点到下午 6 点。

B：Wonderful. But my Eddie is too young，and I'm worried if he can adapt to the curriculums there.　太好了。但我家埃迪太小了,我担心他能否适应那里的课程。

A：Don't worry. The educators there are qualified and experienced. Nutritious meals and snacks are provided.　别担心。那里的教师都是有教师资质的,并且经验丰富。那里还提供营养餐和零食。

B：Really? That's great. I will contact the child-care center this afternoon.　真的吗? 那太棒了。我今天下午就联系这家托儿所。

2. **Words and Expressions** 单词和词组

（1）energetic　/ˌenəˈdʒetɪk/　*adj*．精力充沛的,积极的,有力的

（2）stay up　熬夜

（3）midnight　/ˈmɪdnaɪt/　*adj*．半夜的

（4）as a matter of fact　事实上

（5）sleepless　/ˈsliːplɪs/　*adj*．失眠的,不休息的

（6）year-round　/ˈjɪəˈraʊnd/　*adj*．整年的,一年到头的

（7）adapt　/əˈdæpt/　*v*．适应

（8）qualified　/ˈkwɒlɪfaɪd/　*adj*．合格的,有资格的

（9）experienced　/ɪkˈspɪərɪənst/　*adj*．富有经验的,老练的,熟练的

（10）nutritious　/njʊˈtrɪʃəs/　*adj*．有营养的

（11）snack　/snæk/　*n*．小吃,点心

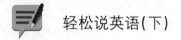

3. Tips and Notes　要点解释

（1）as a matter of fact 和 in fact 结构不同，但意思一样，都表达事实上。它们用法相同，可以在口语或书面语中替换使用。如：Jim is late today. As a matter of fact/In fact，he's late every day.　吉姆今天迟到了。事实上，他每天都迟到。

（2）对话中出现的 seldom 是频度副词，类似的还有 always、usually、never 等。它们的意思不同，按照频率高低排列是：always 总是，usually 通常，often 经常，seldom 不常、偶尔，never 从不。具体要根据事件发生的频率来使用。

4. Drills　句型操练

（1）As a matter of fact ...

As a matter of fact，she is a walking dictionary.

As a matter of fact，he is the only one to solve this problem.

As a matter of fact，we were just talking about you when you came in.

（2）Why not ...?

Why not go shopping with us?

Why not let her do as she likes?

Why not do something that interests you?

（3）I'm worried if ...

I'm worried if he can pass the exam.

I'm worried if we can catch the early bus.

I'm worried if she can get used to the life there.

5. Recitation   常用句背诵

（1）What's up?   怎么啦？

（2）I'm worried if he can adapt to the curriculums there.   我担心他能否适应那里的课程。

（3）Let me think for a while.   让我想一会儿。

6. Follow Up   拓展学习

Rice Kindercare

Kara Ross
Center Director

181 County Road B2 W
Roseville, MN55113

(651) 490-1403

Ages: 6 weeks to 5 years
Open: 6:30 a.m. to 6:00 p.m., M-F

TUITION & OPENINGS

Programs Offered:

- Infant Programs (6 weeks-1 year)
- Toddler Programs (1-2 years)
- Discovery Pre-school Programs (2-3 years)
- Pre-school Programs (3-4 years)
- Pre-kindergarten Programs (4-5 years)
- Summer Programs (pre-school, pre-kindergarten, and school-age)

Accreditations:
- NAEYC

Distance from address: 1.32 miles

Rice Kindercare

卡拉罗斯
中心主任

181 County Road B2 W
Roseville, MN55113

(651) 490-1403

年龄：
　　6周至5岁
开放时间：
　　周一至周五，
　　上午6:30至下午6:00

学费和招生课程

提供的课程：
- 婴儿课程（6周-1岁）
- 幼儿课程（1-2岁）
- 发现学前课程（2-3岁）
- 学前课程（3-4岁）
- 幼儿园课程（4-5岁）
- 暑期课程（学前班、幼儿园班和学龄班）

资质认证：
- NAEYC

路程：1.32英里

Ⅱ. Picking up Kids　接送孩子

1. Dialogues　对话

A=Mrs.Zhang　张太太；B=Neighbour　邻居

A：How time flies! Next month，Eddie is going to begin his kindergarten life.　时光飞逝！下个月埃迪就要开始上幼儿园了。

B：That's good news. It means Eddie will have a new school life.　这是好消息。这意味着埃迪要开始他全新的学校生活了。

A：Yeah. But I have another headache. The kindergarten is a bit far from our community. It will take us about half an hour to walk there. You know I have no driving licence and can't send him to school in a car. 对的。但我有另一件头痛的事。幼儿园离我们社区有点远，步行大约要半个小时。您知道，我没有驾照，不能开车送孩子上学。

B：Don't worry. School buses are provided for free in all kindergartens. What you need to do is to send Eddie to the designated stop at a stipulated time in the morning and pick him up at a set time in the afternoon. 别担心。所有的幼儿园都免费提供校车。您需要做的就是早上在规定的时间把埃迪送到指定的接送点，下午在固定的时间接他回家。

A：It's fantastic. Then I will have more free time. 这太棒了。这样我就有更多的自由时间了。

B：Yes. But remember to arrive at the designated stop on time，and 5 minutes earlier will be better. It's not polite to be late. 没错。请记得要准时到达指定的接送点，提前 5 分钟会更好。迟到是不礼貌的。

A：You are right. That means if Eddie wants to take the school bus，he has to get up early. 您说得很对。那就意味着如果埃迪要坐校车的话，他必须要早起了。

B：That's the fact. But children will get used to the change more quickly than we think. 确实。但是孩子们很快就会适应这种变化。

A：I see. Maybe I can also try car pooling. 我明白。也许我还可以试一试拼车。

B：It's a wonderful idea. Good luck. 这个主意不错。祝您好运！

2. Words and Expressions　单词和词组

(1) kindergarten　/ˈkɪndəˌɡɑːt(ə)n/　*n*.　幼儿园,幼稚园

(2) headache　/ˈhedeɪk/　*n*.　令人头痛之事,麻烦,头痛

(3) licence　/ˈlaɪsns /　*n*.　执照,许可证

(4) driving licence　驾驶执照,驾照

(5) for free　免费

(6) designate　/ˈdezɪɡneɪt/　*v*.　指定,指派,标出

(7) designated　/ˈdezɪɡneɪtɪd/　*adj*.　指定的,特指的

(8) stipulate　/ˈstɪpjʊleɪt/　*v*.　规定,保证

(9) stipulated time　规定时间

(10) fantastic　/fænˈtæstɪk/　*adj*.　极好的,奇异的,空想的

(11) car pooling　拼车,汽车共乘

3. Tips and Notes　要点解释

You know I have no driving licence and can't send him to school in a car.　您知道,我没有驾照,不能开车送孩子上学。

句中的 in a car 相当于 by car。英语中交通工具前用 by 时,不能加冠词,如:by bus/bike/ship/plane/car/taxi ...,但是如果用其他介词,交通工具前要加上冠词或代词进行修饰,如:on the bus、in his car、on a bike 等。

4. Drills　句型操练

(1) It takes me/him/her/you/them/us some time to do ...

It will take you one hour to walk there.

It takes me nearly one hour to make a cake.

It took them many years to build a bridge for the villagers.

（2）What you need to do is to ...

What you need to do is to find your hobbies.

What you need to do is to do as the teacher told you.

What you need to do is to meet more people and make more friends.

（3）take (good) care of ...

Please take care of yourself.

The nurse takes good care of the patients.

The parents took good care of their children.

5. Recitation　常用句背诵

（1）How time flies!　时光飞逝!

（2）I have another headache.　我有另一件头痛的事。

（3）5 minutes earlier will be better.　提早 5 分钟更好。

6. Follow Up　拓展学习

Why Are School Buses in Canada the Safest in the World?
为什么加拿大的校车是全球最安全的?

Uniform School Bus Code All Over Canada

School buses are the safest transport means for kids in Canada. Besides the strict rules, the uniform standard ensures the safety of the kids in terms of hardware. The colour, pattern and equipment are all uniform. Bright yellow colour is striking; the school buses look strong enough, a little like armored cars. From

Apr.1, 2006 on, the newly-built school buses are furnished with fixing buckles to the safety seats to make sure kids under 18 kg are safer when taking the school bus.

全加拿大统一校车规范

校车是加拿大最安全的儿童运输工具,除法规严格外,全加拿大统一的规范标准从硬件上保障了儿童的安全。加拿大校车颜色、款式和配备都是统一的。校车鲜艳的黄色非常醒目,外形看起来很结实,有点像装甲车。从 2006 年 4 月 1 日起,新制造的校车要配备安全座椅的固定扣,以确保体重未满 18 kg 的儿童乘坐校车时更加安全。

Priority to the School Buses

It's explicitly stipulated in Canadian traffic rules that when the school bus stops, emergency red light flashes with a "STOP" cross-bar out, all the vehicles behind the school bus must stop until the red light goes out and cross-bar is in. Whoever breaks the rules will be fined as well as have a bad driving record. Such strict traffic rules show the great care of the society to the kids.

交通法规保障校车优先通行权

加拿大的交通法明确规定,当校车停下来,紧急红灯闪烁,车内伸出有"STOP"字样的横杆时,校车后面的所有车辆都必须停下。直到校车上的紧急红灯熄灭,横杆收回去了,方可前进。如果有人敢以身试法,不但会被罚款,还会被计入不良驾驶记录。这样严厉的交通法规,体现了加拿大社会对儿童的极大关爱。

Ⅲ. Unable to Pick up the Child on Time
不能按时接孩子

1. Dialogues　对话

A=Susan's Grandma 苏珊的奶奶；B=Ms. Martin 马丁女士

A：Good afternoon，Ms. Martin. I'm afraid that I can't pick up Susan on time this afternoon.　下午好，马丁女士。恐怕我今天下午不能按时去接苏珊了。

B：Oh，what happened?　哦，发生什么事了吗？

A：My puppy is seriously ill and I am taking it to see the vet. 我家的小狗病得很重，我正带它去看病。

B：I'm sorry to hear that. But children under 13 are not allowed to go home alone.　很抱歉听到这个消息。但是 13 岁以下的孩子不允许独自回家。

A：That's why I'm calling you. Can Susan stay in her classroom for another one hour after school?　这就是我打电话给您的原因。苏珊放学后能否在教室里多待 1 个小时呢？

B：One hour? I have to remind you that in Canada it will be fined for picking up children late. And it will be C＄6 for one minute.　1 个小时？我必须提醒您，在加拿大接孩子迟到是要被罚款的，1 分钟 6 加币。

A：My goodness. I now come to understand why picking up the children is always the first thing in Canada.　天哪！现在我明白了为什么在加拿大接孩子是一件天大的事。

B：One more thing I have to tell you is to remember to contact

65

us before hand if there is an emergency. 我还有一件事需要提醒您,如果有急事记得提前联系我们。

A: Got it. I'll try my best to get to the school before 5 p.m. I hope it's my last time to be late for picking up Susan. 听懂了。我会尽力在下午5点前到达学校。希望这是我最后一次晚接苏珊。

B: That's good. You are expected to pick up Susan before 5 p.m. Bye. 很好。希望您5点前能来接走苏珊,再见。

2. Words and Expressions 单词和词组

(1) puppy /ˈpʌpɪ/ n. 小狗,幼犬

(2) vet /vet/ n. 兽医

(3) remind /rɪˈmaɪnd/ v. 提醒,使想起

(4) fine /faɪn/ v. 罚款,澄清; n. 罚款

(5) one more thing 还有一件事

(6) before hand 事先,预先

(7) emergency /ɪˈmɜːdʒ(ə)nsɪ/ n. 紧急情况,突发事件

(8) be expected to 被期待,有望,应该

3. Tips and Notes 要点解释

(1) But children under 13 are not allowed to go home alone. 但是13岁以下的孩子不允许独自回家。

本句中涉及 allow 的用法,allow sb. to do sth.意为允许某人做某事,在本句中用的是被动否定形式,sb. be not allowed to do sth.意为某人不被允许去做某事。如:Pets are not allowed to come into the shops. 宠物不允许进入商店。对话中类似的句子还有:You are expected to pick up Susan before 5 p.m. 希望您5点前能来接

走苏珊。原句是：We expect you to pick up Susan before 5 p.m.

（2）another one hour 意为多待 1 个小时，等同于 one more hour。注意在短语中 another 放在数词之前，而 more 放在数词之后。如：Give me another 10 minutes and I'll solve the problem. 相当于 Give me 10 more minutes and I'll solve the problem.　再给我 10 分钟，我就可以解出这道难题。

（3）I now come to understand why picking up the children is always the first thing in Canada.　现在我明白了为什么在加拿大接孩子是一件天大的事。

这句话中的 come to understand 是指开始明白、渐渐了解。如：I have come to understand the significance of your work.　我想我已渐渐了解了您的工作的意义。

4. Drills　句型操练

（1）be not allowed to ...

You are not allowed to smoke here.

Teenagers are not allowed to go to internet cafes.

Bob is not allowed to play games until he finishes his homework.

（2）That's why ...

That's why I came here.

That's why she gave up the chance.

That's why they looked angry and shouted at you.

（3）You are expected to ...

You are expected to come here at 7 a.m.

You are expected to say "Thank you" when you receive a gift.

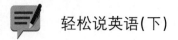

You are expected to be dressed in a formal way when attending a party.

5. Recitation　常用句背诵

(1) What happened?　发生什么事了吗?

(2) But children under 13 are not allowed to go home alone. 但是 13 岁以下的孩子不允许独自回家。

6. Follow Up　拓展学习

I'm Leaving to Pick up My Child

It's one past four o'clock in the afternoon. The ushers were getting off work and said "We don't want to work overtime. We're leaving to pick up our kids." The judge asked, "If you all leave, who can ensure my safety? Let's go together." The lawyers for the prosecution and defense asked, "Then what can we do?" "Why not discuss it tomorrow? I'm leaving to pick up my child too." The judge answered as he took off his robe.

我要去接孩子了

时间是下午 4:01，庭警们要下班了，他们说："我们可不想加班，我们得去接孩子了。"法官问："你们都走了，谁来保护我的安全? 我们一起走吧!"检方和辩方律师问："那我们怎么办?"法官一边脱下法袍一边回答："那就明天再讨论吧，我也要去接孩子了。"

Unit 6 Going to the Beach
去海边

Ⅰ. Going Surfing 去冲浪

1. Dialogues 对话

A=Friend A 朋友 A；B=Friend B 朋友 B

A：What a lovely day. Let's enjoy a sunbath on the beach. 天气真好！我们在海滩上享受一下日光浴吧！

B：Terrific idea. There are so many pleasure-seekers lying themselves flat on the beach to enjoy the sunbath. I guess it must be relaxing. 很棒的主意。有很多游客躺在海滩上享受日光浴呢。我想那一定很放松。

A：You'll feel completely relaxed. But don't forget to apply some sunscreen before the sunbath in case of sunburn. 您会感觉彻底放松。在享受日光浴前不要忘记涂些防晒霜，以免被晒伤。

B：You are right. Let's apply sunscreen first and wear sunglasses. 您说得对。我们先涂些防晒霜，再戴上太阳镜。

（One hour later 1个小时后）

B：Oh，I love the beach，I love sunbath. I'm fully relaxed and I feel sleepy. 哦，我喜欢海滩，我喜欢日光浴。我感觉身心放松，都有点想睡觉了。

A：The waves are very big. Do you want to go surfing? I'm sure it's exciting.　浪这么大,您想去冲浪吗? 我保证很刺激。

B：Is today's weather suitable for surfing?　今天的天气适合冲浪吗?

A：Yes，it is safe today.　是的,今天很安全。

B：Which part of the beach is the safest place to surf?　在这片海滩,哪里冲浪最安全?

A：About 10 minutes' walk to your left.　往您的左边走大约 10 分钟就可以到。

B：Is there a life guard on duty?　有救生员值班吗?

A：Yes，from 8 a.m. to 4 p.m. As far as I know, it is very safe if you don't go far.　有的,他们的工作时间是从上午 8 点到下午 4 点。据我所知,如果您不去太远的话是很安全的。

2. Words and Expressions　单词和词组

(1) surf　/sɜːf/　*v.*　冲浪

(2) go surfing　去冲浪

(3) sunbath　/'sʌnbɑːθ/　*n.*　日光浴

(4) terrific　/tə'rɪfɪk/　*adj.*　极好的,极其的

(5) pleasure-seeker　/'pleʒə'siːkə(r)/　*n.*　游客,追求享乐的人

(6) sunscreen　/'sʌnskriːn/　*n.*　防晒霜

(7) apply some sunscreen　涂抹防晒霜

(8) sunburn　/'sʌnbɜːn/　*n.*　晒黑,/皮肤/晒斑; *v.*　晒伤,晒黑,晒红

(9) life guard　救生员

（10）on duty　值班

（11）as far as I know　据我所知

3. Tips and Notes　要点解释

（1）I guess it must be relaxing.　我猜那一定很放松。

本句中的 must 为情态动词，意为一定，表达肯定的推测，不能翻译为必须。如：She must be very hungry because she ate up all the food.　她一定饿坏了，因为她把食物都吃光了。根据不同的推测语气用不同的情态动词，如 might 也许、could 可能、can't 不可能等。

（2）as far as I know　据我所知

as far as 可以作从属连词，意为就……来说、在……范围内，强调程度或范围。如 as far as I see、as far as I'm concerned 相当于 so far as，意为就……而言、就……来说。as far as 还可以作介词短语或连词，意为像……那样远、远到……，强调至某一指明地点或距离。如：You can see as far as the coast.　极目远眺，您能看到海岸。

4. Drills　句型操练

（1）There is/are ... doing ...

There is a plane flying in the sky.

There are some boys playing basketball there.

There are some people singing happily in the park.

（2）Which ... is the safest（place）to surf?

Which park is the nearest to go?

Which season is the best to go travelling?

Which gift is the most meaningful to give to my grandson?

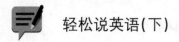
（3）What's the problem?

What's up?

What's wrong with you?

What's the matter with you?

5. Recitation 常用句背诵

（1）Terrific idea. 很棒的主意。

（2）About 10 minutes' walk to your left. 往您的左边走大约 10 分钟就可以到。

（3）Is everything ready? 都准备妥当了吗？

6. Follow Up 拓展学习

The Beach 海滩(诗)

Come to the beach

Where the sea is blue

天蓝蓝，来到海滩上

And little white waves

Come running at you

浪花卷起

A wave comes splashing

Over your toes

从脚趾间穿过

You just stand still

静静站立

And away it goes

看着浪花离去

We will build a castle

Down by the sea

我们来造一个城堡

And look for shells

寻找贝壳

If you come with me

和我一起

Ⅱ. Sea Sports　海上运动

1. Dialogues　对话

A＝Friend A　朋友 A；B＝Friend B　朋友 B

A：Would you like to try water-skiing? You only need to stand on the board which is pulled by a motorboat.　想不想试一试滑水？您只需要站在滑板上，前面有汽艇牵引。

B：Just like a sled pulled by dogs? I'm not sure if I dare to have a try. But I'm willing to watch you ski. Look，there's a billboard which indicates the ski access lane.　就像狗拉雪橇一样吗？我不确定自己敢不敢尝试。但是我愿意看您滑水。看，那里有一个指示牌，上面有去滑水通道的方向指示。

A：Yes，let's follow the direction arrow.　是的，我们按指示方向走。

B：It's the safety caution. I will take some photos of you while you are skiing. So just enjoy yourself.　这是安全注意事项。您滑水的时候我帮您拍些照片，玩得开心！

（Half an hour later　半个小时后）

B：Wow, you are a perfect water-skier. As a spectator and photographer, I feel excited. I have taken a lot of pictures for you. 哇,您真是一个完美的滑水运动员。作为一名观众和摄影师,我觉得很兴奋。我给您拍了很多照片。

A：Thanks a lot. It's fun skiing on such a fine day. Why not go swimming in the sea? 非常感谢。在这么好的天气里滑水真是太有乐趣了。为什么不去海里游泳呢?

B：Swimming is my favourite. I used to swim in the swimming pool. Are there any differences to swim in the sea? 游泳是我的最爱。我过去常常在游泳池里游泳。在海里游泳有什么不同吗?

A：I prefer to swim in the sea because the sea water is more buoyant than the fresh water. Moreover, you can enjoy the beautiful scenery when you swim in the sea. 我喜欢在海里游泳,因为海水的浮力比淡水大。而且,在海里游泳还可以欣赏美丽的景色。

B：That's true. What style of swimming do you like best? 没错。您最喜欢什么泳姿?

A：I like back stroke best. How about you? 我最喜欢仰泳。您呢?

B：I usually swim freestyle stroke as it keeps me from getting tired easily. 我通常自由泳,因为自由泳不容易累。

A：Have you brought your bathing suit, towels and swimming goggles with you? 您有没有带上泳衣、浴巾和泳镜?

B：Of course, I have. I can't wait to swim in the sea and enjoy the scenery of the sea. 当然。我迫不及待地想去海里游泳,欣赏大海的美景。

2. Words and Expressions　单词和词组

（1）water-ski　/'wɔtəskɪ/　v.　滑水

（2）motorboat　/'məutəbəut/　n.　摩托艇,汽船,汽艇

（3）billboard　/'bɪlbɔːd/　n.　布告板,广告牌

（4）indicate　/'ɪndɪkeɪt/　v.　表明,指出

（5）access　/'ækses/　n.　通道,通路

（6）lane　/leɪn/　n.　小路,跑道

（7）access lane　进出路径,出入车道

（8）arrow　/'ærəu/　n.　箭,箭头,箭头记号

（9）caution　/'kɔːʃ(ə)n/　n.　小心,谨慎,警告,警示

（10）spectator　/spek'teɪtə/　n.　观众,旁观者

（11）photographer　/fə'tɒɡrəfə/　n.　摄影师,照相师

（12）buoyant　/'bɔɪənt/　adj.　有浮力的,轻快的

（13）stroke　/strəuk/　n.　游泳姿势

（14）back stroke　仰泳

（15）freestyle　/'friːstaɪl/　n.　自由式

（16）freestyle stroke　自由泳

（17）bathing suit　泳衣

（18）goggle　/'ɡɒɡ(ə)l/　n.　游泳镜,护目镜,眼镜

（19）can't wait to do　等不及去做,迫不及待

3. Tips and Notes　要点解释

（1）You only need to stand on the board which is pulled by a motorboat.　您只需要站在滑板上,前面有汽艇牵引。

本句中 which is pulled by a motorboat 是定语从句,修饰先行词 the board。类似的句子还有:"I suppose the skipper is the person

75

who steers the motorboat."其中,who steers the motorboat 是定语从句,修饰先行词 the skipper。

(2) ... on such a fine day.　在这么好的天气里……

英语中使用介词时应注意:具体某一天或者某个上午、下午、晚上用介词 on。如 on a rainy day 在雨天、on a cold morning 在一个寒冷的早晨、on Thursday afternoon 在星期四的下午。

such 意为如此,修饰名词。要注意 such 和 so 的区别。修饰形容词或者副词时用 so,如... on such a fine day 相当于... on so fine a day,意为在这么好的天气里……"He is such a kind man."相当于"He is so kind a man."意为他是这么好的一个人。

4. Drills　句型操练

(1) I'm not sure if I/you/she/he/they ...

I'm not sure if you can join us.

I'm not sure if he is the right person for this job.

I'm not sure if they have made the correct decision.

(2) It's fun doing ...

It's fun swimming in the sea.

It's fun going surfing on such a fine day.

It's fun playing Tai Ji in the park every morning.

(3) It's a pity that ...

It's a pity that she failed in the test.

It's a pity that you didn't come yesterday.

It's a pity that he missed the chance to see you.

5. Recitation　常用句背诵

（1）Would you like to try water-skiing?　想不想试一试滑水？

（2）So just enjoy yourself.　玩得开心！

（3）Why not go swimming in the sea?　为什么不去海里游泳呢？

（4）I can't wait to swim in the sea and enjoy the scenery of the sea.　我迫不及待地想去海里游泳，欣赏大海的美景。

6. Follow Up　拓展学习

Safety on the Water
水上安全须知

First，take and wear a lifejacket.

第一，拿好并穿上救生衣。

Second，be a responsible skipper，because the skipper has to keep everyone safe.

第二，做一名负责的"船长"，确保自己及他人的安全。

Third，carry a means of communication，such as a mobile phone，flares or beacons.

第三，带上通信工具，如手机、信号弹或者警示灯。

Fourth，reduce the speed when you are close to the shore.

第四，在靠近海岸时减慢速度。

Last but not the least，no alcohol before water-skiing.

第五，滑水前不要饮酒。

Ⅲ. About Toilets　关于洗手间

1. Dialogues　对话

A＝Arthur　亚瑟；B＝Tony　托尼

A：Excuse me, Tony, where's the WC? I wanna pee.　打扰一下，托尼，厕所在哪里？我想小便。

B：WC? We seldom use that word. It means "Water Closet". WC？我们很少用那个词。它的意思是"抽水马桶"。

A：I'm sorry, I mean "toilet".　对不起，我是指洗手间。

B：Look at that white house, that's a public toilet, and you can answer the call of nature there.　看那座白色的房子，它是一个洗手间，您可以去解决一下内急。

A：Thank you, I'll be back soon.　谢谢，我很快就回来。

（A few minutes later　几分钟后）

A：Hi, Tony, I want to tell you what I found in that toilet. It's more than a toilet because you can take a shower inside. And it's really clean.　嗨，托尼。我想要说一说我在那个洗手间里看到的情况。它不仅仅是一个洗手间，您还可以在里面淋浴，而且真的很干净。

B：Is it unisex?　是男女混用的吗？

A：No, no, of course not. Men's Room and Women's Room are separate.　不，不，当然不是。有男洗手间和女洗手间。

B：Ha-ha, I was pulling your leg. But do remember the word "toilet" should not be used randomly. For example, when you are a guest to somebody's home, you can only use "bathroom"; if you go to the KFC, you'd better use "washroom".　哈哈,我只是开个玩笑。但是一定要记得不能随意使用"toilet"这个单词。举个例子,当您被邀请去别人家做客时,您只能用"bathroom"表示洗手间;如果您去肯德基,最好用"washroom"来指代。

A：Can I use the word "toilet" when I take a plane?　我乘坐飞机时可以用"toilet"这个单词吗?

B：The fact is you'd better not. If you are on a plane, you can use "lavatory" and at the airport, "restroom" is often used.　最好不要。乘坐飞机时,您可以用"lavatory"表示洗手间,而在机场,则经常用"restroom"。

A：So when can the word "toilet" be used properly?　那什么时候用"toilet"这个单词恰当呢?

B：People usually use "toilet" or "washroom" in public places.　人们通常在公共场所用"toilet"或者"washroom"表示洗手间。

A：Wow, that's really helpful to me so that I will not make a fool of myself.　哇,这对我太有帮助了,这样我就不会闹笑话了。

B：I'm sure you are a quick learner. What's more, when a lady says "I need to powder my nose.", it means she needs to use the powder room, an expression for ladies' room.　我相信您是一个学习能力很强的人。还有一点,当女士说"I need to powder my nose."时,是指她想用一下"化妆间",也就是女厕的意思。

A：Are there any euphemisms for Men's room?　那男厕有没有什么委婉的表达方法?

B：Good question. You can say "I have to go to the John."or "I want to go to the happy room." or "I wanna wash my hands." And all those are more tactful than "I wanna pee."　好问题。您可以说

"I have to go to the John."或者" I want to go to the happy room." 或者 "I wanna wash my hands."。这些都比"I wanna pee."更委婉。

A：I got it. Thank your very much. 我理解了。非常感谢！

2. Words and Expressions　单词和词组

（1）take a shower　淋浴

（2）unisex　/'juːnɪseks/　*adj*. 不分男女的

（3）separate　/(for *adj*.)'seprət，(for *v*.)'sepəreɪt/　*adj*. 单独的，分开的；　*v*. 分开，隔开

（4）randomly　/'rændəmlɪ/　*adv*. 随便地，任意地

（5）lavatory　/'lævət(ə)rɪ/　*n*. 厕所，盥洗室

（6）make a fool of　愚弄，欺骗

（7）euphemism　/'juːfəmɪz(ə)m/　*n*. 委婉语

（8）tactful　/'tæktfʊl；-f(ə)l/　*adj*. 得体的，圆滑的

3. Tips and Notes　要点解释

（1）It's more than a toilet ...　它不仅仅是一个洗手间……

当 more than 后面跟名词的时候，表示不只是，不仅仅是，如：She is more than a teacher to us, she is our friend.　她不只是教师，她还是我们的朋友。

（2）Wow, that's really helpful to me so that I will not make a fool of myself.　哇，这对我太有帮助了，这样我就不会闹笑话了。

本句中的 so that 引导一个结果状语，表示因此，此时不可以用 in order that 代替。so that 引导目的状语时，意为"目的是……"，从句中往往要加上 can/could/may/might 等情态动词，可以用 in order that 代替。如：He got up early so that/in order that he could catch the early bus. 他起得很早，为的是赶上早班车。

4. Drills 句型操练

（1）... so that ...

Bring it nearer so that I may see it better.

The boy often told lies so that nobody believed him.

He injured his left foot so that he was unable to walk.

（2）As is known to all ...

As is known to all，paper was first made in China.

As is known to all，China is still a developing country.

As is known to all，China is a large country with a long history.

（3）Honestly speaking/Frankly speaking/Interestingly enough ...

Honestly speaking，I don't worry about him at all.

Frankly speaking，you are not the right person to do this job.

Interestingly enough，she likes pets now though she used to dislike them.

5. Recitation 常用句背诵

（1）You can answer the call of nature there. 您可以去解决一下内急。

（2）I was pulling your leg. 我只是开个玩笑。

（3）I need to powder my nose. 我想用一下"化妆间"。（女士用语）

（4）I have to go to the John./I want to go to the happy room./I wanna wash my hands. 我想去一下洗手间。（男士用语）

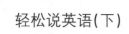

6. Follow Up 拓展学习

Different Toilet Signs 不同的厕所标识

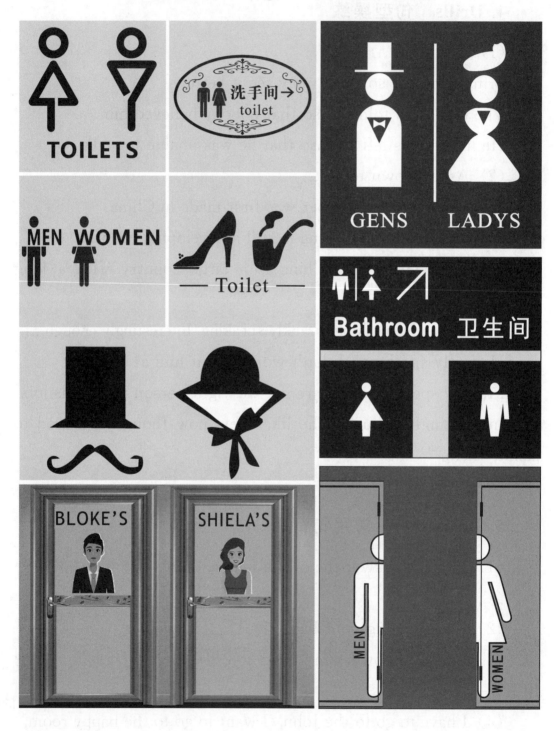

Unit 7　About Travelling
有关旅行

Ⅰ. Introduction of Surroundings　环境介绍

1. Dialogues　对话

A＝A Neighbour 邻居；B＝Mrs. Smith 史密斯太太

A：Hi，Mrs. Smith. I intend to climb mountains this weekend. Do you have any recommendations?　您好，史密斯太太。我打算这个周末去爬山，您有什么推荐吗？

B：Why not go to Blue Mountains National Park? It is located in the west of Sydney and about two hours' drive from here.　为什么不去蓝山国家公园呢？它位于悉尼的西边，大约两个小时的车程。

A：Terrific. Why is it called Blue Mountains? Is it because the mountains are blue?　太好了。为什么它叫作蓝山？是因为山是蓝色的吗？

B：No. It's just because of the eucalyptus trees.　不。这是因为桉树。

A：Eucalyptus trees? I know their leaves are known as the favourite food of koalas.　桉树？我知道桉树的叶子是考拉最爱的食物。

B：You are right. Nearly 90 kinds of eucalyptus trees grow in

83

Blue Mountains and they give off a pleasant smell. With the reflection of the sunshine, the mountains look blue. 您说得没错。蓝山有大约 90 种桉树，它们散发出好闻的香味，在阳光的反射下，整座山笼罩在蓝色的氤氲中。

A：It must be very beautiful there. 那里一定很漂亮。

B：Absolutely. If you go there, don't miss the iconic place——the Three Sisters. 绝对漂亮。如果您去那里，不要错过标志性景点——三姐妹峰。

A：I guess there will be some good sites for me to see them. 我想那里肯定还有很多观景点。

B：That's true. One of the best places to get a view of them is Echo Point. But you can enjoy a different view if you take a cable car. 确实。其中一个最佳的观景点是回声角。但是如果您乘坐缆车，您又可以看到不同的风景。

A：It's a good idea. Where can I take it? 这个主意好。我在哪里可以乘坐缆车呢？

B：Scenic World in Katoomba, where you can take Skyway, Railway and Cableway. 在卡通巴的景观世界，您可以乘坐空中缆车、悬崖快车和空中索道。

A：Does that mean I have to take 3 different kinds of cable cars? What are the differences? 这是不是意味着我要乘坐三种不同的缆车？它们有什么不同之处？

B：Yes. If you want to appreciate the views better, just take Skyway, the highest cable car in Australia. You can see the Three Sisters and Katoomba Falls in the cable car. 是的。如果您想有更好的观赏体验，不妨乘坐空中缆车，它是澳大利亚最高的缆车。您可以坐在缆车中观赏三姐妹峰和卡通巴瀑布。

A：Fantastic. Is there anything particular in Railway and Cableway?　好棒啊！那悬崖快车和空中索道有什么特别之处呢？

B：Both Railway and Cableway provide the biggest cable cars，holding 84 passengers in one car. And they are the steepest in the world with an inclination angle of 52 degrees.　悬崖快车和空中索道都是世界上最大的缆车，每车可以容纳 84 名乘客，它们也是世界上最陡峭的缆车，有 52°的倾斜角。

A：That will be an exciting and extraordinary experience. I'm looking forward to it.　这将是一种激动人心而又不同寻常的体验。我很期待！

2. Words and Expressions　单词和词组

（1）be located in　位于，坐落在

（2）eucalyptus　/ˌjuːkə'lɪptəs/　n．桉树

（3）be known as　以……著称，被称为

（4）koala　/kəʊ'ɑːlə/　n．树袋熊（考拉）

（5）give off　散发出

（6）reflection　/rɪ'flekʃ(ə)n/　n．反射

（7）absolutely　/'æbsəluːtlɪ/　adv．绝对地，完全地

（8）iconic　/aɪ'kɒnɪk/　adj．标志性的

（9）get a view of　看到……的景象

（10）echo　/'ekəʊ/　n．回声

（11）cable　/'keɪb(ə)l/　n．缆绳，电缆

（12）scenic　/'siːnɪk/　n．风景胜地；　adj．风景优美的

（13）falls　/fɔːls/　n．瀑布

（14）fantastic　/fæn'tæstɪk/　adj．极好的，奇异的

（15）steep /stiːp/ *adj.* 陡峭的

（16）inclination /ɪnklɪˈneɪʃ(ə)n/ *n.* 倾斜,斜坡

（17）angle /ˈæŋɡ(ə)l/ *n.* 角,角度

（18）extraordinary /ɪkˈstrɔːdənrɪ/ *adj.* 非凡的,特别的

3. Tips and Notes 要点解释

（1）about two hours' drive 大约两个小时的车程

这里的 two hours' 相当于一个形容词,翻译为两个小时的,可以用 two-hour 来代替。类似的短语有:30 minutes' walk 相当于 30-minute walk,意为 30 分钟的步行;five years' hard work 相当于 five-year hard work,意为 5 年的辛勤工作。

（2）It's just because of the eucalyptus trees. 这是因为桉树。

这里的 because of 表示因为,但和 because 不一样。because of 是复合介词,后面加名词(短语)、代词或动名词,如:He lost his job because of his age. 由于年龄关系他失去了工作。而 because 是连词,后面跟从句。如:He lost his job because that he was too old. 由于年龄关系他失去了工作。

（3）I know their leaves are known as the favourite food of koalas. 我知道桉树的叶子是考拉最爱的食物。

这句话中的 be known as 翻译为以……著称、被称为。要注意它和 be known for 以及 be known to 的区别。be known for 翻译为因为……而著名,be known to 翻译为对……来说著名。如:She is known to many young people as a singer for her songs. 作为一名歌手,她的歌曲对年轻人来说很著名。

（4）Is there anything particular in Railway and Cableway? 那悬崖快车和空中索道有什么特别之处呢?

形容词修饰不定代词 something、anything、nothing、somebody、nobody 等时，应该放在不定代词的后面。如：Is there anything strange?　有什么奇怪的吗? I have something important to tell you.　我有一些重要的事要告诉您。

4. Drills　句型操练

（1）… because (of) …

She was late because it rained.

She was late because of the rain.

He walked slowly because of his injured leg.

（2）… is/are known as/for …

Kunming is known as the Spring City.

Shanghai is known as the magic city.

Chengdu is known for its delicious snacks and hot pot.

（3）I/She/He/They/We will be doing …

I will be having a holiday this time next week.

She will be lying on the beach this time next month.

What will you be doing at 6 o'clock tomorrow evening?

5. Recitation　常用句背诵

（1）It must be very beautiful there.　那里一定很漂亮。

（2）I am sure I will be screaming with excitement.　我肯定会激动地尖叫。

（3）I'm looking forward to the coming of this weekend.　我盼望着周末的来临。

6. Follow Up 拓展学习

To Plan a Trip to Australia 计划去澳大利亚旅行

A＝Visitor 参观者；B＝Travel Agent 旅行社接待员

A：What is the language of Australia? 澳大利亚人使用什么语言？

B：Australia's official language is English. However，Australia is a multicultural nation with a significant migrant population，so it's common to hear a diverse range of languages in Australia's cities and towns. 澳大利亚的官方语言是英语。然而,澳大利亚是一个拥有大量移民人口的多元文化国家,因此在澳大利亚的城镇中听到各种语言是很常见的。

A：Is tipping customary in Australia? 在澳大利亚付小费是惯常做法吗？

B：Hotels and restaurants do not add service charges to your bill，and tipping is always your choice. In upmarket restaurants，it is common to tip waiters 10 percent of the bill for good service. 酒店和餐馆不会将服务费加入您的账单,是否付小费取决于您自己。在高档餐厅,人们通常会因优质的服务向服务员支付账单金额的10％作为小费。

A：Can I bargain prices in Australia? 我可以在澳大利亚讨价还价吗？

B：No. It is not customary to bargain in Australia. 不。澳大利亚一般没有讨价还价的习俗。

A：What is the emergency number in Australia? 澳大利亚的紧急电话号码是多少？

B：The emergency number for police，ambulance and fire

brigade is 000.　警察、救护车和消防队的紧急电话号码是 000。

A：Is it safe to swim in Australia's waters?　在澳大利亚的水域游泳是否安全?

B：Australia's popular beaches are usually patrolled by volunteer lifesavers from October to April and red and yellow flags mark the safest area for swimming.　救生员志愿者会于每年 10 月至下一年的 4 月在澳大利亚颇受欢迎的海滩进行巡逻，而有红旗和黄旗标志的游泳区是最安全的。

Ⅱ. Rainforest Features　雨林特色

1. Dialogues　对话

A＝Visitor 参观者；B＝Native Citizen 当地居民

A：Kuranda Rainforest is said to be the paradise of animals and plants. I'm considering having a trip there.　据说库兰达热带雨林是动植物的天堂。我正考虑去那里一趟。

B：If you want to have a chance to get close to a wide range of animals，birds and plants，Kuranda Rainforest will be the best choice.　如果您想找个机会去接近各种各样的动物、鸟类和植物，库兰达热带雨林是不二之选。

A：Really? I have been to many rainforests before. Are there any features about this rainforest?　真的吗? 我之前去过很多雨林，这个雨林有什么特色吗?

B：It will satisfy all your imagination about rainforests. It's the oldest rainforest on the earth. Because of the relatively isolated surroundings，many ancient species，including some endangered

89

species，survive. 它能满足您对雨林的所有想象。它是地球上最古老的雨林。由于它相对独立的环境，很多古老物种，包括濒临灭绝的物种都保存了下来。

A：Unbelievable. I am sure that I will keep my eyes wide open so as not to miss anything. 难以置信！我相信我一定会把眼睛睁得大大的，不错过任何事物。

B：You certainly will. If you want to take a photo with a koala，the Koala Garden will satisfy you. 您肯定会的。如果您想和考拉拍照，考拉园肯定能满足您。

A：I will take my camera and take as many photos as possible. 我要带上相机，尽可能多拍一些照片。

B：Furthermore，if you are interested in the cultures of Australian aboriginals，the trip to Kuranda will be meaningful to you. 此外，如果您对澳大利亚原住民文化感兴趣的话，这趟库兰达之行对您来说一定会颇有意义。

A：Terrific. It's reported that their unique dancing，musical instruments and coloured drawings have been in the world cultural heritage list. 太好了。据说他们独特的舞蹈、乐器和彩绘已经被列入世界文化遗产名录了。

B：In a word，the trip to Kuranda will enable you to enjoy both nature and culture. 总而言之，这趟库兰达之行将会给您带来自然和文化的双重享受。

2. **Words and Expressions** 单词和词组

（1）rainforest /'reinfɒrist/ *n.* （热带）雨林

（2）get close to 靠近，接近

(3) relatively /ˈrelətɪvlɪ/ *adv.* 相对地,相当地

(4) isolated /ˈaɪsəleɪtɪd/ *adj.* 孤立的,偏远的

(5) surroundings /səˈraʊndɪŋz/ *n.* 环境

(6) ancient /ˈeɪnʃənt/ *adj.* 古代的,古老的

(7) species /ˈspiːʃiːz/ *n.* 生物,物种

(8) endangered /ɪnˈdeɪndʒəd/ *adj.* 濒临灭绝的

(9) survive /səˈvaɪv/ *v.* 幸存,生还

(10) unbelievable /ʌnbɪˈliːvəb(ə)l/ *adj.* 难以置信的

(11) aboriginal /æbəˈrɪdʒɪn(ə)l/ *n.* 土著居民; *adj.* 土著的,原始的

(12) unique /juːˈniːk/ *adj.* 独特的,稀罕的

(13) instrument /ˈɪnstrʊm(ə)nt/ *n.* 乐器

(14) heritage /ˈherɪtɪdʒ/ *n.* 遗产

3. Tips and Notes 要点解释

(1) be said to do 据说、be believed to do 被认为,类似的还有 be reported to do 据报道、be thought to do 被认为。它们可以改写成: It's said that …, It's believed that…, It's reported that …, It's thought that …如:据说他下周去伦敦。可以翻译为:"He is said to go to London next week.",也可以翻译为:"It's said that he is going to London next week."。

(2) I am sure that I will keep my eyes wide open so as not to miss anything. 我相信我一定会把眼睛睁得大大的,不错过任何事物。

这句话中的 wide 是副词,修饰 open。wide 既可以作形容词也可以作副词,表示宽的、充分地。widely 是副词,表示广泛地,如:

English is widely used in the world. 英语在全世界广泛应用。so as not to 是 so as to 的否定句,类似的还有 in order not to,翻译为 "为了不……"。动词不定式的否定一律在 to 的前面加 not。

4. Drills 句型操练

(1) ... is said to ...

She is said to be very rich.

They are said to leave very soon.

Women are said to be more emotional than men.

(2) I'm considering ...

I'm considering changing my job.

He is considering moving to the countryside.

We are considering keeping a cat and a dog as pets.

(3) It's reported that ...

It's reported that the president will visit Russia next week.

It's reported that most seniors have a habit of getting up early.

It is reported that housing prices will continue to rise next year.

5. Recitation 常用句背诵

(1) I am sure that I will keep my eyes wide open so as not to miss anything. 我相信我一定会把眼睛睁得大大的,不错过任何事物。

(2) In a word, the trip to Kuranda will enable you to enjoy both nature and culture. 总而言之,这趟库兰达之行将会给您带来

自然和文化的双重享受。

（3）That must be very interesting. 那一定非常有趣。

6. Follow Up　拓展学习

Amazon Rainforest Travel Guide and Tips

（1）Travel Guide

Unless you have friends living in the Amazon，it is a brilliant idea to hire a tourist guide! Being lost in the wilderness is no fun!

（2）Tips and Warnings

• Respect the customs and traditions as well as the privacy of the Amazonian tribes. Before clicking photographs of the tribal people，ask for their permission.

• Do not approach or touch the wildlife. And please avoid littering.

• No matter what time of year you visit，it is advised to get yourself vaccinated before your trip to the Amazon rainforest. Check with your doctor and get appropriate medicines as well. You are advised to get yourself vaccinated for hepatitis and yellow fever. Also check up on antimalarial medicines.

• Do check out the credentials of the tourist guides you opt for.

• Even if you are a hiker，please don't miss an opportunity to see the rainforest by boat. It is an experience of a lifetime.

• A unique ecosystem flourishes in the Amazon. Remember that you are visiting a place where the laws of the nature govern. Always stay close to your guides and groups.

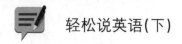

亚马逊雨林旅行指南和技巧

（1）旅游指南

除非您有朋友住在亚马逊，否则还是建议您明智地请一个导游！迷失在荒野中并不是一件有趣的事！

（2）提示和警告

· 尊重亚马逊部落的习俗、传统以及隐私。在拍摄部落人的照片之前，请征得他们的同意。

· 不要靠近或接触野生动植物。不乱扔垃圾。

· 无论您何时来访，都建议您在前往亚马逊雨林之前接种疫苗。请咨询医生并获取适当的药物。建议您接种肝炎和黄热病疫苗。您还需要了解抗疟疾药物。

· 请确认您所选的导游的资质。

· 即使您是徒步旅行者，也请不要错过乘船观赏热带雨林的机会。这将会是让您一生难忘的经历。

· 亚马逊雨林里有独特的生态系统，欣欣向荣。请记住，您正在访问的地方，一切都遵循着大自然的规律。请始终跟紧您的导游和团队。

Ⅲ. Hot Springs　温泉

1. Dialogues 对话

A＝Receptionist 接待员；B＝Peter 彼得

A：Good afternoon，Hepburn Bathhouse & Spa. What can I do for you?　下午好，这里是赫本洗浴和水疗中心。我能为您做点什么吗？

B：Good afternoon. I plan to have a spa with my wife next

weekend in Daylesford.　下午好。我计划下个周末和我的妻子来戴尔斯福德泡一下温泉。

A：OK. Can I have your name please?　好的，可以告诉我您的名字吗？

B：Peter，P-E-T-E-R.　彼得，拼写为 P-E-T-E-R。

A：Thank you. By the way，which hot spring do you prefer, the indoor spring or the outdoor spring?　谢谢。您偏好哪种温泉，室内的还是室外的？

B：I have no idea. Can you make some suggestions?　我不太了解。您能给我一些建议吗？

A：The indoor spring is connected to the outdoor spring. You can try the indoor spring before you go outdoors and enjoy the view.　室内温泉连着室外温泉。您可以在泡完室内温泉后，再到露天温泉，一边泡一边欣赏风景。

B：Perfect idea. Is there a hot spring that is only for individuals or the family? I hope to have a more pleasant and comfortable experience.　好主意！有供个人或者全家单独使用的温泉吗？我希望能够有更舒适的体验。

A：Yes. We have relaxation pools, salt bath physiotherapy pools, and fragrant steam rooms, which are more suitable for private or unique experiences.　有的。我们有放松室、盐浴理疗室、芳香蒸汽室。在这些地方，您可以享受私人空间，获得独特的体验。

B：It sounds terrific.　听起来很不错！

A：Well，our spa has the longest history in this area. Tourists can enjoy the best spa here because our hot springs contain high mineral content and a wide variety of supreme service is offered.　我们的温泉水疗中心是这个地区历史最为悠久的水疗场所。水质好，富含矿

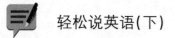

物质,并提供多种优质服务,游客们在这里可以享受顶级水疗。

B：No wonder many friends of mine recommended your bathhouse to me. Do I need to pay in advance?　难怪我的很多朋友都向我推荐你们。我需要提前支付吗?

A：No，you needn't. And we will reserve a physiotherapy pool for you.　不需要。我们会帮您预留一个理疗室。

B：That's so kind of you. Thank you，and see you next weekend.　太好了! 谢谢您,下周末再见。

2. Words and Expressions　单词和词组

(1) hot spring　温泉

(2) bathhouse　/'bɑːθhaʊs/　*n.*　浴室,公共澡堂

(3) spa　/spɑː/　*n.*　温泉浴场,水疗会所

(4) indoor spring　室内温泉

(5) outdoor spring　室外温泉

(6) be connected to　与……相连

(7) relaxation　/ˌriːlækˈseɪʃ(ə)n/　*n.*　放松,缓和,消遣

(8) physiotherapy　/ˌfɪzɪəʊˈθerəpɪ/　*n.*　物理疗法

(9) fragrant　/'freɪɡrənt/　*adj.*　芳香的,愉快的

(10) mineral　/'mɪnərəl/　*adj.*　矿物的,矿质的

(11) supreme　/suːˈpriːm; sjuːˈpriːm/　*adj.*　最高的,至高的

(12) no wonder　难怪

(13) reserve　/rɪˈzɜːv/　*v.*　留出,预订

3. Tips and Notes　要点解释

(1) Is there a hot spring that is only for individuals or the

family? 有供个人或者全家单独使用的温泉吗？

这里的 that is only for individuals or the family 为定语从句，修饰 a hot spring。类似的表述有：This is a hot spring that/which can help people relax. 这是一个能帮助人们放松的温泉。

（2）No wonder many friends of mine recommended your bathhouse to me. 难怪我的很多朋友都向我推荐你们。

recommend 意为推荐、建议，后常跟从句、名词、动名词等。如：我推荐他读这本书，可以翻译为："I recommend that he (should) read this book.""I recommend him this book.""I recommend this book to him." "I recommend reading this book."。

4. Drills 句型操练

（1）By the way, which ... do you prefer, ... or ...?

By the way, which colour do you prefer, red or green?

By the way, which kind of song do you prefer, popular or classic?

By the way, which room do you prefer, the double room or the single room?

（2）Do I need to ...?

Do you need to have a rest here?

Does he need to ask for some help?

Does the room need to be cleaned every day?

（3）How expensive it is!

How delicious the food is!

How fast he cooks the dinner!

How terrible the weather looks!

5. Recitation　常用句背诵

(1) I have no idea. Can you make some suggestions?　我不太了解。您能给我一些建议吗?

(2) Do I need to pay in advance?　我需要提前支付吗?

(3) How much do you charge?　收费是多少?

6. Follow Up　拓展学习

BBQ in Australia

The Australians enjoy entertaining their family or friends in their backyards where they have plenty of space and privacy to celebrate an occasion or just because it's a beautiful day. Barbeques (BBQ) in Australia are not just a way to cook food but a way of life.

Most people in Australia are lucky enough to have a back yard and many of these back yards are designed to have BBQ and a swimming pool as the summers here can be long. Almost every house has a BBQ.

In Australia, the BBQ is mainly men's job. There is always much delicious food to cook on your BBQ. Beef, lamb, pork, sausages of all flavors, kebabs of all types ... and the results are fantastic. People here like their steaks big and the food plentiful.

在澳大利亚烧烤

澳大利亚人喜欢在他们的后院聚会,在那里他们享有足够的空间和隐私,以庆祝某个事件,或仅仅为了度过美好的一天。澳大利亚的烧烤不只是一种烹饪方式,更是一种生活方式。

澳大利亚的夏季很长,因而大多数人都很幸运地拥有一个配备烧烤设施和游泳池的后院。几乎每家每户都拥有烧烤设施。

　　在澳大利亚,烧烤主要由男性负责。有很多美味的食物可以用来烧烤。烤牛肉、羊肉、猪肉、不同口味的香肠、各种各样的肉串……简直太棒了! 那里的人们喜欢大块的牛排和丰富的食物。

Unit 8   Outbound Travel
出境游

手机扫码
听单词和对话

Ⅰ. Package Tours   跟团游

1. Dialogues   对话

A＝Travel Agent 旅行社接待员；B＝Visitor 参观者

A：Good morning, Dream Travel Agency. Can I help you?   早上好,这里是梦想旅行社。我能为您做点什么吗?

B：Yes. I'm planning a trip to America. Can you recommend some package tours?   是的。我正计划去美国旅行。您能为我推荐一些跟团游吗?

A：Sure. How much time do you plan to spend in this trip?   当然可以。您计划花费多长时间旅行?

B：10 days. Do you have any recommendations?   10 天。您有什么推荐的吗?

A：America is such a big country that it's impossible to travel to all the places within 10 days. So do you have any particular places in mind?   美国很大,不可能在 10 天内玩遍所有地方。您有没有什么特别想去的地方呢?

B：Yellowstone National Park. It has been my dream place since I was a child.   黄石国家公园。这是我从孩提时代起就梦想去

的地方。

A：Good choice. Yellowstone National Park is located in the west of America. I suggest you have a trip to the west of America.　不错的选择。黄石国家公园位于美国的西部，我建议您来一次美国西部游。

B：Umm，I prefer natural scenery.　嗯，我更喜欢自然景观。

A：OK. How about this route? We will depart from Los Angeles，go through Mojave Desert，and then visit Antelope Canyon and Horseshoe Bend，both of which are the wonderful sites for taking pictures.　好的。我建议从洛杉矶出发，穿过莫哈维沙漠，然后游览羚羊彩穴和马蹄湾，这两处地方都是摄影的绝佳地点。这条路线怎么样？

B：Fantastic. I once saw some pictures of Antelope Canyon in the magazine. It is among the world top 10 photography sites. I think it will be a good chance to improve my skills of taking pictures.　太棒了。我曾经在杂志上看过羚羊彩穴的图片。它还是世界十大摄影地点之一。我觉得这是提高我摄影水平的好机会。

A：I'm sure you will take a lot of wonderful pictures there.　我相信您一定会在那里拍出很多很棒的照片。

2. Words and Expressions　单词和词组

（1）outbound　/'aʊtbaʊnd/　*adj.*　出港的，驶向外国的

（2）package tour　跟团游

（3）have ... in mind　想到，考虑

（4）scenery　/'siːn(ə)rɪ/　*n.*　风景，景色

（5）depart　/dɪ'pɑːt/　*v.*　出发，离开

（6）desert　　/ˈdezət/　　*n*.　沙漠

（7）canyon　　/ˈkænjən/　　*n*.　峡谷

（8）bend　　/bend/　　*n*./*v*.　弯曲

（9）the world top 10　　世界排名前十

3. Tips and Notes　要点解释

（1）America is such a big country that it's impossible to travel to all the places within 10 days.　美国很大，不可能在10天内玩遍所有地方。

此处的 such ... that ... 意为"如此……以至……"，such ... that ... 与 so ... that ... 意思一样，但是 such 后面跟名词，so 后面跟形容词或副词。如：such a big country that ... 相当于 so big a country that ....

（2）It has been my dream place since I was a child.　这是我从孩提时代起就梦想去的地方。

本句中有一个典型的现在完成时结构。当从句用 since 引导，表达自从……时，主句一律用现在完成时。如：I have worked in this city since I came here 10 years ago.　自从我10年前来到这里，我就一直在这座城市工作。

4. Drills　句型操练

（1）How many/much ... will ...?

How many cities will you visit?

How many scenic spots will be visited?

How much time will you spend in travelling?

（2）I/She/He/We/They prefer(s) ...

I prefer a package tour.

She prefers to have a package tour.

We prefer a package tour to an independent tour.

（3）I'm sure you will …

I'm sure you will have a good time there.

I'm sure you will find your trip very interesting.

I'm sure you will take a lot of wonderful pictures there.

5. Recitation　常用句背诵

（1）Do you have any recommendations?　您有什么推荐的吗?

（2）Do you have any particular places in mind?　您有没有什么特别想去的地方呢?

（3）It has been my dream place since I was a child.　这是我从孩提时代起就梦想去的地方。

6. Follow Up　拓展学习

Top 10 Travel Tips for Seniors

Planning a fun, safe, and comfortable trip is simple and easy to do. By following a few travel planning tips, potential disasters or misfortunes can be avoided.

- Select an Aisle Seat on Long Flights
- Keep Medicines Handy
- Print and Share Your Travel Documents
- Know What to Expect on Your Trip
- Navigate the Airport with Ease
- Skip the Alcohol and Drink Lots of Water
- Don't Be Afraid to Ask Crew Members for Help

- Have Healthy Snacks On Hand
- Stand Up and Stretch Often
- Get Help with Your Luggage

老年人旅行的十大建议

规划有趣、安全、舒适的旅行简单易操作。只要遵循一些旅行计划原则,就可以避免潜在的意外或不幸。

- 选择长途航班上靠过道的座位
- 随身携带药物
- 打印并分享您的旅行证件
- 知道旅行中有哪些值得期待的地方
- 到达机场时间充裕
- 不喝酒,多喝水
- 不要害怕向乘务人员寻求帮助
- 手头备好健康零食
- 经常站立和伸展
- 搬运行李时向他人求助

Ⅱ. About Itinerary　讨论行程

1. Dialogues　对话

A＝Visitor A 参观者 A；B＝Visitor B 参观者 B

A：Before going to Yellowstone National Park，We will visit Arches National Park and Great Salt Lake. They are also the classic natural scenery.　在去黄石国家公园前,我们要去游览拱门国家公园和大盐湖,它们也是经典的自然景观。

B：Yeah，I heard of Great Salt Lake when I was a pupil. It's

said that the water in Great Salt Lake is 6 times saltier than the sea water, just like the Dead Sea. 是的,我上小学时就听说过大盐湖,据说大盐湖里面的水比海水要咸 6 倍,就像死海一样。

A：That's true. And we will stay in Salt Lake City for one night. 是这样的。我们将会在盐湖城住一个晚上。

B：Is there any possibility that we stay in Yellowstone National Park for one night? 我们有机会在黄石国家公园住一个晚上吗?

A：Yes. We will spend 2 days touring Yellowstone National Park and stay in Yellowstone overnight. On the following days, we will visit Grand Teton National Park, Bryce Canyon National Park, and Zion National Park. 有的。我们有两天时间游览黄石国家公园,并且会在里面住一个晚上。接下来的几天,我们还将游览大提顿国家公园、布莱斯峡谷国家公园和锡安国家公园。

B：Wow, that would be a visual feast. 哇,那将是一场视觉盛宴。

A：That's right. After touring different parks, we will pay a visit to the Chocolate Factory, do some shopping in Tanger Outlets, have a San Francisco City Tour and finally return to Los Angeles. 没错。在游览完不同的公园后,我们要去参观巧克力工厂,在唐格奥特莱斯购物中心购物,游览旧金山,最后返回洛杉矶。

B：It seems to be a tight and full schedule. After all, I just want to have a trip to relax myself rather than get exhausted. 这个行程似乎太紧凑了,毕竟我只想度个假去放松一下而不是变得精疲力竭。

A：Yes, it's actually a full schedule. Here is another route. It's only an 8-day trip. And San Francisco City Tour is omitted in this route. 也对,这的确是一份很紧凑的行程安排。这里还有另一条路

线,是一个 8 天的行程,里面不含旧金山的游览。

B:Sounds reasonable. I like this itinerary.　听起来很合理。我喜欢这个行程。

2. Words and Expressions　单词和词组

(1) itinerary　/aɪˈtɪn(ə)(rə)rɪ; ɪ-/　*n.*　旅行日程,路线

(2) classic　/ˈklæsɪk/　*adj.*　经典的,古典的

(3) overnight　/əʊvəˈnaɪt/　*adv.*　在夜间,一夜之间

(4) visual　/ˈvɪʒʊəl/　*adj.*　视觉的

(5) feast　/fiːst/　*n.*　宴会

(6) pay a visit to　参观,访问

(7) after all　毕竟

(8) rather than　而不是

(9) omit　/ə(ʊ)ˈmɪt/　*v.*　省略,删除

3. Tips and Notes　要点解释

(1) ... 6 times saltier than ...　比……咸 6 倍

这是一个比较级结构,如果要表达程度或者具体的倍数等,都需要直接放在比较级前面。如:He looks much happier than before.　他看上去比以前开心多了。The prices of the fruits here are twice cheaper than those in the supermarket.　这里水果的价格比超市便宜两倍。

(2) rather than 不与 would 连用时,表示客观事实,意为"是……而不是……、与其……不如……",它连接的并列成分可以是名词、代词、形容词、介词(短语)、动名词、分句、不定式、动词等。如:He is an artist rather than a painter.　与其说他是一名画家,不如说他是一名艺术家。You rather than I are going to have a trip.　是您

106

而不是我要去旅行。We will have the meeting in the classroom rather than in the great hall. 我们是在教室里开会，而不是在大厅里。

4. Drills 句型操练

(1) It's said that ...

It's said that he was cheated by his partner.

It's said that the singer will give a concert next month.

It is said that spending time with animals is good for your health.

(2) It /She /He seems to ...

It seems to be the place that I have been looking for.

She seems to be very happy today.

He seems to have made a lot of friends here.

(3) For a person who ...

What do you suggest for a person who is crazy about fishing?

For a person who loves animals, keeping a pet at home is a good idea.

For a person who likes helping others, it's wise to be a community volunteer.

5. Recitation 常用句背诵

(1) That would be a visual feast. 那将是一场视觉盛宴。

(2) It seems to be a tight and full schedule. 这个行程似乎太紧凑了。

(3) Sounds reasonable. 听起来很合理。

6. Follow Up   拓展学习

American Roadside Inns for the Aged

In America, many aged travellers are interested in self-driving tour. Roadside inns are closely related to the travelling pension. They were used only for parking or luggage left, charging by hour. Since the aged travellers are more welcome there, they are now called roadside inns for the aged.

One of the specialties is that all the staff there are old people who have received short-term training which includes local customs, vehicle maintenance, basic massage and psychology. Since the inns were opened, many old people have driven their cars there specially and enjoyed the service.

美国的路边老人客栈

美国有众多开车自驾游的老年游客,有一种客栈与旅居养老息息相关。这就是设在公路旁边的老人客栈。这类客栈本是为自驾车游客泊车或提供行李安顿服务的简易旅馆,按小时收费,因尤其欢迎老年人来客栈内休息而闻名,简称为路边老人客栈。

这类客栈的一大特色是其中的工作人员均为受过短期业务培训的老年人。培训内容包括当地风土人情、车辆保养知识、基本按摩知识、心理学知识等。自建立以来,许多老年人专门驾车来路边老人客栈,享受温馨的服务。

Mobile Apartments

Travelling by Recreational Vehicle (RV) is very common. There are a great number of good RV campgrounds in many countries. In Australia, many old couples can be seen drinking tea or having a rest beside their RV. For them, the RV is their mobile home and the time on road is their pleasant leisure time.

移动的晚年公寓

房车出游是国外常见的旅居养老出行方式,这得益于许多国家有数量众多、品质出色的房车营地。在澳洲公园式的营地里,经常能看见头发花白的夫妻俩悠然地坐在房车外喝茶休憩,对于他们来说,房车就是移动的家,路上的生活就是怡然自得的养老时光。

Ⅲ. Negotiation on Tour Fees 旅行团费协商

1. Dialogues 对话

A=Travel Agent 旅行社接待员;B=Visitor 参观者

B: How much is the package tour? 全包团费是多少?

A: It's $1,888 per person for this 8-day tour to the west of America. And the fees cover food, accommodation and transportation. But some charged items will be borne by yourself. 这趟为期 8 天的美国西部游,单人费用是 1,888 美元。费用包含所有饮食、住宿和交通费。但是一些自费项目得由您自己承担费用。

B: It is not favorable at all. 这个价格一点儿也不优惠。

A: Maybe you can choose another package tour, it is much cheaper, you only have to pay $688 for the same itinerary. 也许您可以选择另一种跟团游,价格要便宜很多。同一旅游行程只需688 美元。

B: Wow, such a big difference in price. What is covered in the fees? 哇,这么大的价格差距。这笔费用中含有哪些内容?

A: The accommodation in the hotels, Los Angeles airport drop-off and the chartered buses during the 8 days. 酒店的住宿、

洛杉矶机场的送机以及这 8 天的交通包车。

B：That means I have to book the round-trip air tickets by myself. 这就是说我得自己订购往返机票。

A：More than that. Besides the big transportation，meals during the 8 days and the service charge are not covered in the tour fees. You have to pay for them separately. 还不止。除了大交通，8 天内的饮食费以及服务费也不包括在团费中。您需要额外支付。

B：Oh，then I can decide what to eat during the trip for myself. 哦，那我可以自己决定旅行期间吃什么了。

A：If you prefer to have a trip more freely，I recommend you have a DIY tour. 如果您喜欢更自由的行程，我推荐您来一次自由行。

B：Sounds interesting. Do I need to schedule everything? 听起来很有意思。我需要自己安排一切吗？

A：Don't worry. The fees will cover the transportation and accommodation. That's to say，the return air tickets and the hotels will be booked by us. 不用担心。这个团费包括交通费和酒店住宿费。也就是说，往返机票和酒店住宿都由我们来预订。

B：And what do I need to do then? 那我需要做些什么？

A：Just taste the local specialty and try the local transportation. 品尝当地特色菜，感受当地的交通。

B：That's what I have been expecting. I think I can also rent a car to enjoy the scenery better. What is the tour fee? 那正是我一直期待的。我觉得我还可以租一辆车，更好地欣赏美景。团费是多少呢？

A：It's ＄1,088 for each person. 每人 1,088 美元。

B：OK. I can't wait to enjoy this trip. 好的，我等不及要去享

受这次旅行了。

2. Words and Expressions　单词和词组

（1）cover　/'kʌvə/　*v*．包括,覆盖；　*n*．封面

（2）transportation　/trænspɔː'teɪʃ(ə)n/　*n*．交通,运输

（3）charge　/tʃɑːdʒ/　*v*．要价,收费；　*n*．费用

（4）charged item　收费项目,自费项目

（5）favorable　/'feɪvərəbl/　*adj*．优惠的,有利的

（6）airport drop-off　送机

（7）charter　/'tʃɑːtə/　*v*．包租

（8）chartered bus　包车

（9）round-trip　往返航程,往返行程

（10）separately　/'sep(ə)rətlɪ/　*adv*．分别地,个别地

（11）DIY tour　自由行,自主游

（12）that's to say　也就是说

（13）return air tickets　往返机票,回程票

（14）book　/bʊk/　*v*．预订,登记

（15）specialty　/'speʃ(ə)ltɪ/　*n*．特产,招牌菜

（16）rent　/rent/　*v*．租用,租借,出租

3. Tips and Notes　要点解释

（1）I recommend you have a DIY tour.　我推荐您来一次自由行。

这是一个 recommend 引导的从句。当用 recommend、suggest、advise、order 等引导从句时,从句要用虚拟语气,即 recommend/suggest/advise/order that sb. should do sth.,其中的 that 和 should

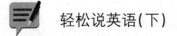

可以省略。如：I suggest (that) he (should) go to see a doctor. 我建议他去看一下医生。

（2）That's what I have been expecting. 那正是我一直期待的。

本句中 what 引导的是一个表语从句，注意用陈述语序。have been doing 是现在完成进行时，表示动作从过去发生到现在，今后还可能继续下去。如：I have been doing the housework the whole morning. 我一整个上午都在做家务（下午可能还要做下去）。

4. Drills　句型操练

（1）... prefer to ...

She prefers to be alone.

I prefer to get around by bike.

More and more people prefer to live in the countryside.

（2）I/She/He/They recommend/suggest/advise/order that ...

He suggests that I go to the concert with him.

I recommend that my son should buy this T-shirt.

They ordered that all the rubbish (should) be cleared within 2 hours.

（3）That's what/why/how/where ...

That's why she comes here.

That's how he learned English in our school.

That's where we are going to have our holiday.

5. Recitation　常用句背诵

（1）Such a big difference in price. 这么大的价格差距。

（2）That's what I have been expecting. 那正是我一直期待的。

（3）I can't wait to enjoy this trip.　我等不及要去享受这次旅行了。

6. Follow Up　拓展学习

Tips for DIY Tour Abroad

（1）Where to go?

If you plan to have a trip abroad，the capital and country should be included in your travel plan. The National Museum in the capital can give you a general idea of the history or cultures of this country and travelling in the country can enable you to experience the real life and enjoy charming views.

（2）How to book flight tickets?

Surf the official website of the airline at least 3 months ahead of your schedule so that you can buy the tickets at a lower price. But some special fares are often not refundable.

（3）Where to live?

Before travelling in a foreign country，you'd better book hotels on line in advance. Decide the scenic spots first and then search the location in the map，look for the nearby hotels and make a comparison.

Bed and Breakfast （BNB） is now a new fashion. If you want to experience the local people's life，BNB will be your first choice.

国外自助游攻略

（1）去哪儿旅游?

如果您有出国旅游的计划,首都和乡镇应该列入您的旅游计划。首都的国家博物馆可以让您对这个国家的历史或文化有一个大致的

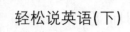

了解,而在乡镇旅行可以让您体验真实的生活,欣赏迷人的风景。

(2)在哪里买机票?

至少提前 3 个月在航空公司的官网检索,您或许可以买到便宜的机票。但有些特价机票是不可以退订的。

(3)住在哪里?

在出国旅游前,最好在线上订好酒店。首先决定自己要去的景点,搜索景点所在位置,然后通过地图寻找附近酒店进行对比选择。

民宿现在是一种新潮流。如果您希望体验当地人的生活,民宿将是您的不二选择。

Unit 9   Living Abroad
客居他乡

Ⅰ. Renting a House   租房

1. Dialogues   对话

A＝Tenant 租客；B＝The Real Estate Agent 房产中介

A：Good morning, I learned that you have apartments for rent. Can I have a look?   早上好,我听说您这儿有公寓要出租,我能看一看吗?

B：Yes. We have a two-room apartment only 300 dollars a month.   可以。我们有两室一厅的,每月只需 300 美元。

A：I'd like to have a look.   我想看一看。

B：OK. We can take you to see the apartment now.   好的。我们现在就可以带您去看房。

（A few moments later   几分钟后）

A：Ah，a window facing a beautiful park and I can hear the birds singing there.   啊,漂亮的窗户面对着公园,我还能听到小鸟在歌唱。

B：Here is a living room. There is a small kitchen. Next is a bathroom.   这是客厅。那边是一间小厨房。厨房隔壁是卫生间。

A：Not bad! We need an apartment with two bedrooms and a bathroom. I'll take it.   多好啊! 我们需要有两间卧室和一个卫生

间的公寓。我就租它吧。

B：OK. Here is the lease. Please sign here. 这是租约,请在这儿签字。

A：The rent is 300 dollars a month. Does that include gas，electricity and heat? 租金是每月 300 美元。它包括燃气、电和暖气的费用吗?

B：Yes. How long is the lease? 是的。您想租多久?

A：One year. All right. I'll sign it now. Here's 600 dollars. 一年。好的,我这就签字。给您两个月的租金 600 美元。

B：Thank you. Here is your copy of the lease and the key. 谢谢。这是给您的租约副本和钥匙。

A：When can I move in? 我什么时候可以搬进来?

B：Anytime you like. 什么时候都可以。

2. Words and Expressions 单词和词组

(1) rent /rent/ *vt*. 出租

(2) apartment /ə'pɑːtm(ə)nt/ *n*. 公寓,房间

(3) living room 客厅

(4) kitchen /'kɪtʃɪn; -tʃ(ə)n/ *n*. 厨房

(5) bathroom /'bɑːθruːm; -rʊm/ *n*. 卫生间

(6) lease /liːs/ *n*. 租约

(7) sign /saɪn/ *vi*. 签名

(8) include /ɪn'kluːd/ *vt*. 包括

(9) gas /gæs/ *n*. 煤气

(10) electricity /ˌɪlek'trɪsətɪ/ *n*. 电

(11) heat /hiːt/ *n*. 暖气

（12）copy　/ˈkɒpɪ/　*n*.　副本

3. Tips and Notes　要点解释

（1）a two-room apartment 相当于 an apartment with two bedrooms　有两间卧室的公寓

新加坡多用 flat 表示公寓，美国多用 apartment 表示公寓。

a two-room flat 相当于 a flat of two bedrooms　有两间卧室的公寓。

（2）lease a house 相当于 rent a house　租房

常见的租房类型如下：

policy rental housing　政策性租赁房

low-rent housing　廉租房

sharing apartments　合租房

4. Drills　句型操练

（1）I'd like to have a …

I'd like to have a try.

I'd like to have a cup of tea.

I'd like to have one more question.

（2）hear sb. doing …

She heard Tom going upstairs.

We often hear her singing next door.

I hear Miss Wu speaking to a foreigner.

（3）How long …?

How long is the film?

How long have you learned English?

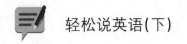

How long have you been a member of the football team?

5. Recitation 常用句背诵

（1）We need an apartment with two bedrooms and a bathroom. 我们需要有两间卧室和一个卫生间的公寓。

（2）Does that include gas, electricity and heat? 它包括燃气、电和暖气的费用吗？

（3）How much is the rent? 租金是多少？

（4）Do you have any smaller and cheaper apartments? 你们有小一点、便宜一点的房子吗？

6. Follow Up 拓展学习

Rent Ad 租房广告

FINCH-WARDEN，lrg 2br bsmt，Lndry，ear-in-kit，w-o balc，close to shops. No smoking/pets，＋，1ˢᵗ/last，222-2222-leave mess. Rent ＄500.

（1）FINCH-WARDEN，这间房位于或邻近 FINCH 和 WARDEN 街交界处。

（2）lrg＝large，2br＝two bedrooms，bsmt＝It is a basement，它位于地库，有两间卧室，很大。

（3）Lndry＝Laundry，它有洗衣机和干衣机。

（4）eat-in-kit＝eat in the kitchen，它的厨房很大，可以在内用餐。

（5）W-o balc＝walk out to a balcony，它有一扇门可通往阳台。

（6）Close to shops，它离商场很近。

（7）No smoking/pets，不接受吸烟或养宠物的租客。

（8）＋，租金以月为单位支付，外加水、电、燃气等费用。

(9) 1ˢᵗ/last,交首尾两个月的租金时还要交定金。

(10) 222-2222-leave mess,打电话给 222-2222,留言联系房东。

(11) Rent ＄500,每个月的租金是 500 美元。

Ⅱ. Inquiring about Local House Rates
询问当地房价

1. Dialogues　对话

A＝Mr. Wang　王先生；B＝Mrs. Wang　王太太；C＝The Real Estate Agent　房产中介

A：Good morning，I'd like to ask something about the house rates.　早上好,我想询问一下当地的房价。

C：Would you tell me what size of the house you're looking for?　能告诉我你想找什么样的房子吗?

B：Let us have a look at these pictures，please.　让我们看一看这些房子的图片吧。(图片略)

A：How about the second picture?　第二张图片(上的房子)怎么样?

B：OK.　不错。

A：May I have a look at it?　我可以看一看吗?

C：Sure. This way，please.　当然可以。请这边走。

A：When was the building built?　它是什么时候建造的?

C：In 2000.　2000 年。

A：The bedrooms facing the south are bright enough. And is there an air-conditioner?　朝南的卧室都很明亮。有空调吗?

C：Yes，it's central air-conditioner. This way，please. This is a big sitting-room. That is a study. Beside the study is a bathroom.　有，是中央空调。请这边走。这是一个大客厅。那是一间书房。书房的旁边是卫生间。

A：Are there any shopping malls and grocery stores nearby?　这附近有大型购物中心和杂货店吗？

C：Yes, of course. There is a Sports Center, too.　当然。还有一家健身中心。

A：How much does it cost?　这套房子要多少钱？

C：353,000 dollars.　35.3 万美元。

B：That's a lot of money. However I like the house. The surroundings are nice and serene.　那是一大笔钱。但我喜欢这套房子，周围环境不错，也很宁静。

A：Can you make it cheaper?　能再便宜一些吗？

C：Take it or leave it. And it's worth that.　就这个价钱，它物有所值。

2. Words and Expressions　单词和词组

（1）rate　/reɪt/　*n.*　价格

（2）air-conditioner　/'eərkənd'ɪʃənər/　*n.*　空调

（3）central air-conditioner　中央空调

（4）study　/'stʌdɪ/　*n.*　书房

（5）shopping mall　大型购物中心

（6）grocery store　杂货店

（7）Sports Center　健身中心

（8）serene　/sɪ'riːn/　*adj.*　宁静的

（9）worth　/wɜːθ/　*prep.*　值……钱

3. Tips and Notes　要点解释

（1）Would you tell me what size of the house you're looking for?　能告诉我你想找什么样的房子吗?

这是一个宾语从句。相似的句子有：Would you tell me what kind of the house you're looking for? Would you tell me what type of the house you're looking for? Would you tell me what sort of the house you're looking for?

（2）the bedrooms facing the south　朝南的卧室

本句中的 facing the south 作定语修饰 the bedrooms，相当于 the bedrooms which face the south。

（3）Take it or leave it.　就这个价钱。

意思是不容讨价还价，类似的表述有：It's the set price.

4. Drills　句型操练

（1）Let us …

Let us see the Sports Center.

Let us have a look at these pictures.

Let us visit the shopping malls and grocery stores.

（2）It's good for …

It's good for your health.

It's good for jogging half an hour every evening.

It's good for planting trees and flowers in March.

（3）It's near …

It's near our workplace.

It's near our grandson's university.

It's near our parents' nursing home.

5. Recitation 　常用句背诵

（1）How about the second picture?　第二张图片（上的房子）怎么样？

（2）The bedrooms facing the south are bright enough.　朝南的卧室都很明亮。

（3）The surroundings are nice and serene.　周围环境不错，也很宁静。

6. Follow Up 　拓展学习

An Apartment of the Two Bedrooms

The big bedroom is neat and clean. There is a large window facing the south. A large desk is against the window. A wardrobe is standing against the wall. There is another smaller room facing the north. There is one bathroom between the two bedrooms. The bathroom is equipped with a shower, a squatting toilet and an electric water heater. The living room is furnished with a TV set, a sofa, a table and four chairs. A lovely balcony lies south of the living room. North of it is a tiny kitchen. There is a sink, a gas stove and a smoke fan in the kitchen.

一套二居室的公寓

大卧室干净整洁，有一个朝南的大窗户。靠窗有一张大桌子，衣柜贴墙而立。朝北是一间小卧室。两个卧室之间有一个浴室。浴室配有淋浴间、蹲式马桶和电热水器。客厅有一台电视机、一张沙发、一张桌子和四把椅子。客厅的南面有一个漂亮的阳台，北面有一个小厨房。厨房里有一个洗碗池、一个燃气灶和一个排烟扇。

Ⅲ. Guest Code and Precautions
客居礼仪及注意事项

1. Dialogues　对话

A=Neighbour 邻居；B=Newcomer 新来者

A：How do you do? You are a newcomer，aren't you?　您好！您是刚搬来的,对吗?

B：Yeah. I am a newcomer here. How do you do?　是的。我刚搬来这儿。您好!

A：For the newcomer，I'm afraid it's better to know something about the guest code and precautions.　新居户最好要了解一下客居礼仪及注意事项。

B：Of course. Please go ahead.　当然需要。请继续讲。

A：First，do not litter. Second，do not spit everywhere. Third，take care of trees，flowers and plants. Fourth，do not cut down the green bushes and trample on the green grass. Fifth，keep voice down especially during late hours. Sixth，keep your room and common area clean and tidy. Seventh，do not deep-fry foods. Eighth，do not push the waste cooking oil into the sink. Ninth，beware that cooking smoke can cause the fire alarm.　第一,不能乱扔垃圾。第二,不能随地吐痰。第三,保护树木、花草。第四,不要砍伐绿色灌木,践踏草坪。第五,保持安静,尤其是在夜深时。第六,保持房间和公共区域整洁。第七,不要烹饪油烟大的食物。第八,不要把菜肴的废油倒进水池里。第九,提防油烟引起火情警报。

B：Thank you very much for telling me so many do's and

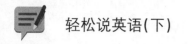

don't s clearly. 十分感谢您告诉我这些注意事项。

2. Words and Expressions　单词和词组

(1) guest code　客居礼仪

(2) precaution　/prɪˈkɔːʃ(ə)n/　*n.*　注意事项,预防措施

(3) newcomer　/ˈnjuːkʌmə/　*n.*　新来者

(4) litter　/ˈlɪtə/　*v.*　扔垃圾

(5) spit　/spɪt/　*v.*　吐痰

(6) trample　/ˈtræmp(ə)l/　*v.*　践踏

(7) deep-fry　/ˈstəfraɪ/　*v.*　油炸

(8) waste　/weɪst/　*adj.*　废弃的

(9) beware　/bɪˈweə/　*v.*　当心,提防

(10) cause　/kɔːz/　*v.*　引起

(11) fire alarm　火情警报

3. Tips and Notes　要点解释

(1) You're a newcomer, aren't you?　您是刚搬来的,对吗?

这是一个反意疑问句。反意疑问句有两种结构。第一种结构为前半句是肯定句,后半句是否定句。如:You're a student, aren't you?　你是一个学生,对吗? 第二种结构为前半句是否定句,后半句是肯定句。如:He isn't a teacher, is he?　他不是一名教师,对吗?

(2) Thank you very much for telling me so many do's and don'ts clearly.　十分感谢您告诉我这些注意事项。

do's and don'ts　行为准则,守则

Restaurant Do's and Don'ts　餐馆须知

More do's and don'ts for parents include: do turn off your

124

phone. 父母需要注意的事项还包括：务必将手机关机。

4. Drills 句型操练

（1）It's better to ...

It's better to go home on foot.

It's better to know something about table manners.

It's better to understand something about the do's and don'ts in the park.

（2）Keep voice down ...

Keep voice down in the library.

Keep voice down as the baby is sleeping.

Keep voice down when the film is going on.

（3）Push ...

Push the litter into the dustbin.

Push the door while entering the bank.

Don't push the waste water into the rivers and seas.

5. Recitation 常用句背诵

（1）For the newcomer，I'm afraid it's better to know something about the guest code and precautions. 新居户最好要了解一下客居礼仪及注意事项。

（2）Keep your room and common area clean and tidy. 保持房间和公共区域整洁。

（3）Beware that cooking smoke can cause the fire alarm. 提防油烟引起火情警报。

（4）Thank you very much for telling me so many do's and

don'ts clearly. 十分感谢您告诉我这些注意事项。

6. Follow Up 拓展学习

Moving Out from the Rental

A＝The Real Estate Agent 房产中介；B＝Mr.Smith 史密斯先生

A：Mr. Smith，I need to inspect the apartment before you move out.

B：No problem. Please come in.

A：I'm afraid I'll have to deduct 30％ of your deposit.

B：Why? What's the matter?

A：Look over here. There are stains on the wall and the flooring is cracked. The lease allows me to withhold your deposit to pay for cleaning and repairs.

B：Please don't. I'll clean and make the necessary repairs before I move out.

A：OK. See you.

搬出租赁房

A：史密斯先生,在您搬出去之前,我得检查一下公寓。

B：没问题,请进。

A：恐怕我得扣除您30％的押金。

B：为什么? 出了什么事?

A：看这里,墙上有污渍,地板嘭啪作响。按照租约,我可以从押金中扣除清洁和修理的费用。

B：请不要这样。在我搬出去之前,我会打扫和做必要的修理工作。

A：好吧。再见。

Unit 10　Handling a Traffic Accident

Unit 10

手机扫码
听单词和对话

处理交通事故

Ⅰ. Asking Help for a Traffic Accident　车祸求助

1. Dialogues　对话

A＝911 Service 911 服务热线；B＝Tourist　游客

A：Hello，this is 911. What can I do for you?　您好，这里是911。我能为您做点什么吗?

B：Yes. We had a traffic accident and one of us was badly injured.　是的。我们发生了车祸，我们中有人受了重伤。

A：Where are you?　你们在哪儿?

B：I don't know where we are. I don't know much English. I come from China. I'm travelling in the U.S.　我不知道我们身在何处。我英语懂得不多。我来自中国，正在美国旅游。

A：Don't worry. Try to find out the place where you are. How about the landmark nearby?　别着急。请看一看周围有没有什么地标，试着找到你们身在何处。

B：Oh，I see a tall building named White Swan Hotel nearby.　哦，我看见附近有一幢大厦，上面写着"白天鹅宾馆"。

A：Good. What about using the mobile's position system to find out your place?　很好。请用手机定位系统查一查你们目前所

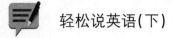

在的位置。

B：Wow，I have no difficulty in finding out our place. We are near the City Park.　哇！我毫不费力地找到我们的位置了。我们在城市公园附近。

A：All right. Stay where you are. The police will arrive soon.　好的。待在原地。警方很快就到。

2. Words and Expressions　单词和词组

(1) traffic　/ˈtræfɪk/　*n*. 交通

(2) accident　/ˈæksɪdənt/　*n*. 事故

(3) badly　/ˈbædlɪ/　*adv*. 严重地

(4) injure　/ˈɪndʒə/　*v*. 伤害

(5) landmark　/ˈlæn(d)mɑːk/ *n*. 地标

(6) swan　/swɒn/　*n*. 天鹅

(7) mobile　/ˈməʊbaɪl/　*n*. 手机

(8) position　/pəˈzɪʃən/　*n*. 位置

(9) system　/ˈsɪstəm/　*n*. 系统

(10) police　/pəˈliːs/　*n*. 警方

3. Tips and Notes　要点解释

(1) a traffic accident　一起车祸、交通事故

a major traffic accident　一起重大的交通事故

a bad traffic accident　一起糟糕的交通事故

其中，accident 强调偶然或意外发生的不幸事件。

(2) What can I do for you?　我能为您做点什么吗？

类似的表述有：Is there anything I can do for you? Can I

help you?

(3) Stay where you are. 待在原地。

相当于 You stay where you are. 这是一个祈使句,省略了主语 you,句中的 where you are 是地点状语从句,修饰动词 stay。

类似的句子有:Stand where you are. Put everything where they are.

4. Drills　句型操练

(1) Hello，this is ...

Hello，this is 911 (110，119，120).

Hello，this is the police station.

Hello，this is Mr. Li's wife，Mrs. Li.

(2) One of ...

One of us is retired.

One of them has passed the driving licence.

One of the foreigners returned to their homeland.

(3) near ...; nearby ...; beside ...

Our school is near my home.

Nearby the City Park are lots of buildings.

There is a shopping mall beside the Sunny Park.

5. Recitation　常用句背诵

(1) We had a traffic accident and one of us was badly injured. 我们发生了车祸,我们中有人受了重伤。

(2) I don't know where we are. 我不知道我们身在何处。

(3) I have no difficulty in finding out our place. 我毫不费力

地找到我们的位置了。

(4) The police will arrive soon. 警方很快就到。

6. Follow Up 拓展学习

A Story

A=Frank 弗兰克；B=A Passer-by 一名路人

(Frank was just robbed by a robber. He is a stranger in this place. He doesn't know what to do.)

A：Help! Help!

B：What happened to you，sir? Are you all right?

A：Robber! I was just robbed! Please call 911 quickly.

B：Wait，wait，please calm down. Any valuables were robbed away?

A：A young man robbed me of my wallet and smart phone just now.

B：Oh，I see. I have dialed 911. Everything will be OK.

A：Thank you. No words can express my gratitude to you.

一则故事

(弗兰克刚刚被一名强盗抢劫。他是一名人生地不熟的游客，不知道该怎么办。)

A：救命啊！救命啊！

B：先生，怎么啦？您还好吧？

A：强盗！我被抢劫了。请快帮我拨打911。

B：等一下，等一下，请镇静一些。您有贵重物品被抢劫了吗？

A：刚才一个年轻人抢了我的钱包和智能手机。

B：哦，我明白了。我已拨打911。一切都会好起来的。

A：谢谢您,真是感激不尽。

Ⅱ. Communicating with Police
与警方交流

1. Dialogues　对话

A＝Policeman 警察；B＝Tourist 游客

（After the policeman arrives　警方来了之后）

A：What happened here?　这儿发生了什么事?

B：We had a traffic accident. A car wanted to overtake ours. It hit our vehicle from behind and drove away.　我们发生了交通事故。一辆车在路上不停地想要超车。它从后面撞上我们的车并逃掉了。

A：Did you stop at a red light?　您在红灯亮时停车了吗?

B：Yes. I'm sure that I did not break the law.　是的。我确信我没有违反交通规则。

A：I see. Did you see the car's plate?　我知道了。您看见那辆车的牌照了吗?

B：I am sorry. I was too much shocked. I remember it was a white car.　很抱歉。我当时惊吓过度以至没有留意到。我只记得它是一辆白色的车。

A：May I see your driver's licence, registration, insurance?　我能看一下您的驾照、车辆登记信息和保险吗?

B：Sure. Here you are.　可以,给您。

A：Good. Is anyone injured?　好的。有人受伤吗?

B：I'm OK, but my friend broke his arm.　我还好,但我的朋

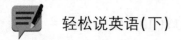

友撞断了胳膊。

A：We'll call an ambulance right now. 我们马上打电话叫救护车。

B：Thank you. Please inform the insurance company for us. And I can't speak much English. I would like to have a translation service. 谢谢。请帮我们给保险公司打一下电话。我不太懂英语，我想请求翻译服务。

A：No problem. 没问题。

2. Words and Expressions 单词和词组

(1) happen /'hæp(ə)n/ *vi*. 发生

(2) hit /hɪt/ *v*. 碰撞

(3) drive away 逃跑

(4) break the law 违反法律

(5) plate /pleɪt/ *n*. 牌照，盘子

(6) registration /redʒɪ'streɪʃ(ə)n/ *n*. 车辆登记信息

(7) insurance /ɪn'ʃʊər(ə)ns/ *n*. 保险

(8) arm /ɑːm/ *n*. 胳膊

(9) ambulance /'æmbjʊl(ə)ns/ *n*. 救护车

(10) translation service 翻译服务

3. Tips and Notes 要点解释

(1) What happened here? 这儿发生了什么事？

注意 happen 后接人时需要加上介词 to，如：What happened to you? What happened to her? What happened to them?

(2) I'm sure that I did not break the law. 我确信我没有违反

交通规则。

break the law 表示违反交通规则，类似的表述有：obey the law 遵守法律；the law of football 足球比赛规则

（3）I was too much shocked. 我当时惊吓过度。

shocked 意为震惊的。如：We were too shocked to talk. 我们愕然无语。Don't look so shocked. 别这么生气。

4. Drills 句型操练

（1）drive away（相当于 run away）

I just saw the car drive away.

You must stay in the car and don't drive away.

My son will drive away my loneliness by talking about interesting things.

（2）I'm sure ...

I'm sure I can win the game.

I'm sure he has passed the final examination.

I'm sure we have not seen each other for more than twenty years.

（3）I（don't）think ...

I think he is injured in the car accident.

I don't think I broke the law by mistake.

I think everyone of us should keep fit.

5. Recitation 常用句背诵

（1）We had a traffic accident. 我们发生了交通事故。

（2）I'm sure that I did not break the law. 我确信我没有违反

交通规则。

（3）May I see your driver's licence，registration，insurance？ 我能看一下您的驾照、车辆登记信息和保险吗?

（4）Please inform the insurance company for us. 请帮我们给保险公司打一下电话。

6. Follow Up 拓展学习

Traffic Jam

A＝Passenger 乘客；B＝Driver 司机

A：Oh，my goodness，the traffic is crawling.

B：I think there's an accident ahead.

A：We're now running late.

B：I know. Why don't we take a different way?

A：Let me have a look at the GPS. Yes，there's an exit 3 miles ahead. We'll exit Market Street，head west，and then get on the Pennsylvania Freeway.

B：OK，let's do that even though we may have to take a detour way.

交通堵塞

A：噢，天哪！车辆行进缓慢。

B：我认为前方可能出事故了。

A：我们要迟到了。

B：我知道。我们为什么不走另外一条路呢?

A：让我看一看 GPS 导航。前方 3 英里处有一个出口。我们从市场街出去，向西走，然后上宾夕法尼亚高速公路。

B：好的，虽然有些绕道，我们还是这样走吧。

Ⅲ. Claims Service of Insurance Company
保险公司理赔

1. Dialogues 对话

A＝Insurance Actuary 保险公司理赔员；B＝Tourist 游客

A：Good morning, sir. Is there anything I can do for you? 早上好,先生,请问有什么事?

B：Good morning. I had an accident with my car. 早上好。我的车子发生了交通事故。

A：Let me see your car. Oh, Something is wrong with the air bag. We'll tow your car to the dump. It's useless. We'll pay you for a new car. How much did you buy your car? 让我看一看您的汽车。车子的安全气囊坏了。我们只能拖去报废厂了。我们会支付您买一辆新车的钱。您购买这辆车花了多少钱?

B：It cost me 50,000 dollars a year ago. 一年前,我花了5万美金。

A：Well, only one year. Then we'll make it 10% discount. That's 45,000 dollars settlement. 喔,仅仅一年。那么,我们给您打个九折。也就是说,赔付您4.5万美金。

B：Thank you very much. This is the bill for the medical treatment of the injured person. 谢谢。这是伤者的看病账单。

A：What size of the car accident personal insurance? 这是什么类型的车祸人身保险?

B：Car accident personal insurance amount is all-inclusive, including the responsible parties and victims. 车祸人身保险的额

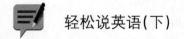

度是全包,包括肇事方和受害者。

A：Then pay in full. 那就是全额赔付。

B：How about the responsible party? He is running away. 那么肇事方怎么处理呢? 他跑掉了。

A：He can not escape from the law. We'll find him and give him a credit rating. 他逃不掉法律的制裁。我们会找到他,并对其进行信用评级。

B：I'm really grateful to you. 真是太感谢了。

2. Words and Expressions　单词和词组

(1) actuary　/ˈæktʃuərɪ/　*n*. 保险计算员,保险精算师

(2) insurance actuary　保险公司理赔员

(3) air bag　安全气囊

(4) tow　/təʊ/　*v*. 拖

(5) dump　/dʌmp/　*n*. 垃圾场,报废厂

(6) discount　/ˈdɪskaʊnt/　*n*. 折扣

(7) settlement　/ˈset(ə)lm(ə)nt/　*n*. 结算

(8) all-inclusive　/ˌɔːl inˈkluːsiv/　*adj*. 包括一切的,包括全部费用的

(9) responsible party　当事人,肇事方

(10) victim　/ˈvɪktɪm/ *n*. 受害者

(11) credit rating　信用评级

3. Tips and Notes　要点解释

(1) Something is wrong with the air bag. 车子的安全气囊坏了。

类似的表述有：There is something wrong with your air bag. Your air bag doesn't work. The car's air bag is broken.

（2）Then we'll make it 10% discount.　那么,我们给您打个九折。

相当于 10 discount on sale。

（3）We'll find him and give him a credit rating.　我们会找到他,并对其进行信用评级。

类似的表述有：take him a credit rating、decide him a credit rating、make a decision for his credit rating。

4. Drills　句型操练

（1）pay for ...

We need to pay for the meal.

I paid ten dollars for the interesting book.

He paid a lot of money for the victim in a traffic accident.

（2）How much ...?

How much is the house?

How much should I tip her?

How much do they pay you monthly?

（3）Say goodbye to ...

Say goodbye to you all.

See you later.

I'll be seeing you.

5. Recitation　常用句背诵

（1）It cost me 50,000 dollars a year ago.　一年前,我花了 5 万

美金。

（2）Then we'll make it 10% discount. 那么,我们给您打个九折。

（3）Car accident personal insurance amount is all-inclusive, including the responsible parties and victims. 车祸人身保险的额度是全包,包括肇事方和受害者。

6. Follow Up　拓展学习

Be Fined Due to Breaking Red Light

A＝Officer 警官；B＝Jack 杰克

A：Excuse me, sir, didn't you see the red light?

B：Oh, I thought I could make a right turn on red here.

A：No, sir. The sign says "No Turn on Red".

B：Oh, I guess I didn't see it.

A：I'm sorry, sir, but may I see your driver's licence and insurance policy, please? I have to give you a ticket.

B：Here you are.

A：Sign here, please. You can appeal to the court within 14 days. This slip has all the information you need. Please drive safely, sir.

B：Thank you, Officer!

因闯红灯而被罚

A：先生,您没有看见红灯吗?

B：哦,我原以为能在红灯前右转的。

A：不,先生,这个标志牌上写着"红灯禁止转弯"。

B：哦,我没看见。

A：不好意思，先生，我可以看一下您的驾照和保单吗？我要给您罚单。

B：给您。

A：请在这儿签字。您可以在 14 天内向法院上诉。这里有您需要的信息。请安全行驶，先生。

B：谢谢您，警官。

Unit 11　Expressing Feelings
情感表达

手机扫码
听单词和对话

Ⅰ. Expressing Satisfaction and Gratitude
表示满意与感谢

1. Dialogues　对话

Satisfaction　满足

A＝Anna 安娜；B＝Jason 杰森

A：Hello，Anna is speaking.　您好，我是安娜。

B：Hi，Anna，this is Jason.　嗨，安娜，我是杰森。

A：Jason! Have you been good?　杰森，您最近好吗？

B：Yes. How are you，Anna?　很好。您怎么样，安娜？

A：I'm fine. What have you been doing?　我很好。您最近在忙什么呢？

B：Working. I got a promotion. I've been really busy these days.　工作。我升职了。这些天我特别忙。

A：That's great. Congratulations!　太好了。恭喜恭喜！

B：Thanks. I'm feeling pretty good about myself，a bigger office，a raise and even an assistant.　谢谢。我自我感觉良好，办公室大了，薪水高了，甚至还配了一名助手。

A：That's good. How do you like your new boss?　不错，您的

新老板怎么样？

B：She's very nice and open-minded. 她人很好，思想也很开明。

A：Much better than the last one，huh？ 比上一个老板好多了，是吧？

B：Yeah，he always made us overwork. 是的，他（上一个老板）总是让我们加班。

A：Forget about him. Come over to my house tonight，let's have a celebration. 忘了他吧。今晚到我家来，我们庆祝一下。

B：OK. 好的。

Gratitude 感谢

A＝Ada 艾达；B＝Susie 苏西

A：Need a hand？ 需要帮忙吗？

B：Um … well，yes. 嗯……是的。

A：What's the problem？ 有什么问题？

B：This copy machine doesn't work. 复印机坏了。

A：Let me have a look at it. Well，it's out of paper. 让我看一看。哦，是没纸了。

B：Thanks a lot. Can you do me a favour？ 谢谢。您可以帮我一个忙吗？

A：Sure. 当然可以。

B：Could you staple these together？ 您能帮忙把这些订在一起吗？

A：No problem. 没问题。

B：Thanks for all your kindness. 谢谢。

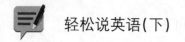
2. Words and Expressions　单词和词组

(1) satisfaction　/ˌsætɪsˈfækʃ(ə)n/　*n*．满足

(2) promotion　/prəˈməʊʃn/　*n*．提升,升职

(3) congratulations　/kənˌɡrætʃəˈleʃənz/　*n*．祝贺

(4) raise　/reɪz/　*n*．加薪

(5) assistant　/əˈsɪst(ə)nt/　*n*．助手

(6) open-minded　/ˈəʊpənˈmaɪndɪd/　*adj*．思想开明的

(7) overwork　/əʊvəˈwɜːk/　*v*．加班

(8) celebration　/selɪˈbreɪʃ(ə)n/　*n*．庆祝

(9) copy machine　复印机

(10) favour　/ˈfeɪvə/　*n*．恩惠

(11) do sb. a favour　帮某人一个忙

(12) staple　/ˈsteɪp(ə)l/　*v*．钉住

(13) kindness　/ˈkaɪn(d)nɪs/　*n*．仁慈,好意

3. Tips and Notes　要点解释

(1) What have you been doing?　您最近在忙什么呢?

本句中的 have been doing 是现在完成进行时,其构成形式是:助动词 have/has been＋动词的现在分词 v-ing。如：I have been working here for three years.　我已经在这里工作 3 年了(表示现在还在这里工作)。现在完成进行时主要用来表达从过去某时开始一直持续到现在的动作,特别强调现在该动作仍在进行。如：It has been raining for three hours.　雨已经下了三个小时。We have been reading an English book for half an hour.　我们已经读了半个小时的英语书。

(2) get a promotion　升职

类似的表述有：sales promotion 促销、health promotion 养生、website promotion 网站推广。

（3）He always made us overwork. 他总是让我们加班。

make/have/let sb. do sth. 让、使、教某人做某事。在主动语态的句子里，这三个使役动词后面的动词前不能加 to，如：Let's have a celebration. 我们庆祝一下。Let me have a look at it. 让我看一看。Let me know if there is anything I can do. 需要帮忙的话就告诉我一声。Don't make the boy cry. 别让这个男孩哭。The teacher will have Tom help Group A. 老师将让汤姆帮助 A 组。

4. Drills   句型操练

（1）... open-minded.

She's very nice and open-minded.

Their boss looks silly and cold-minded.

Miss Nancy is very kind and warm-hearted.

（2）much ＋ 形容词比较级 ＋ than

Much better than the last one.

Much worse than last month.

Much more difficult than the lessons in English Book Two.

（3）It seems that ...

It seems that everything is going well.

It seems that we are working hard at English.

It seems that he enjoys himself in the Olympic Games.

5. Recitation   常用句背诵

（1）What have you been doing?   您最近在忙什么呢？

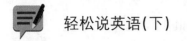

（2）I'm feeling pretty good about myself. 我自我感觉良好。

（3）Can you do me a favour? 您可以帮我一个忙吗？

6. Follow Up 拓展学习

Thank You for Your Help 谢谢您的帮助

A＝Bill 比尔；B＝Mary 玛丽

A：Excuse me，do you know where I can find information on computer? 打扰一下，您知道从哪里能找到关于计算机的信息吗？

B：Yes，of course. These books are in aisle 5. I can take you there. 噢，当然知道。这些书在第五过道处。我可以带您去。

A：Thank you very much for your help. 非常感谢您的帮助。

B：You are welcome. 您太客气了。

A：Can you recommend one for me? 您能帮我推荐一本吗？

B：This one is my favourite. 这本是我最喜欢的。

A：Great. Thanks again for your help! 好极了。再次感谢您的帮助！

Ⅱ. Expressing Displeasure and Regret
表示不愉快与遗憾

1. Dialogues 对话

A＝Annie 安妮；B＝David 大卫

A：David，why don't you clean your room? You look gloomy today. Need someone to talk to? 大卫，您为什么没有清理房间？您今天看起来很郁闷。要找个人聊一聊吗？

B：I'm not in the mood. 我今天没心情。

144

A：Why are you feeling depressed?　您为什么不开心？

B：I was told my wife was speaking ill of me. It's a real letdown.　我听说我的妻子在说我的坏话。这真让人失望。

A：I don't think she would do such a thing.　我觉得她不会做那样的事。

B：But she did and it made me sad. I don't feel like doing anything today.　但她做了，这让我很难过。我今天什么都不想干。

A：Oh, cheer up. Your wife is not everything.　哦，高兴点儿。您的妻子不是您的一切。

B：However she means a lot to me. Who can I turn to in my hour of need like this?　然而她对我很重要。在这种需要帮助的时候，我能向谁求助呢？

A：Then forgive her mistake. You can talk to your parents whenever you are in trouble. And your friend is someone you can turn to when your spirits need a lift.　那就原谅她吧。在遇到困难的时候，您可以向父母求助。在您的精神需要鼓舞时，您可以向朋友求助。

B：Thanks.　谢谢。

2. Words and Expressions　单词和词组

（1）displeasure　/dɪsˈpleʒə/　*n*．不愉快

（2）regret　/rɪˈgret/　*n*．遗憾

（3）gloomy　/ˈgluːmɪ/　*adj*．沮丧的

（4）in the mood　心情好，兴致勃勃

（5）depressed　/dɪˈprest/　*adj*．沮丧的

（6）ill　/ɪl/　*n*．坏话，病人，伤害

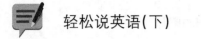

(7) letdown /'letdaʊn/ *n.* 失望

(8) cheer up 高兴点儿

(9) in one's hour of need 在某人需要帮助的时候

(10) forgive /fə'gɪv/ *v.* 原谅

(11) whenever /wen'evə/ *adv.* 无论何时

(12) spirit /'spɪrɪt/ *n.* 精神

(13) lift /lɪft/ *n.* 鼓舞

3. Tips and Notes 要点解释

(1) I'm not in the mood. 我今天没心情。

相当于 I'm in no mood. Not in the mood. I have no mood today.

(2) I was told my wife was speaking ill of me. 我听说我的妻子在说我的坏话。

这是一个主句为被动语态的复合句,里面含有一个宾语从句。被动语态的构成形式是：be+过去分词。本句主句 I was told …,为一般过去时被动语态。

(3) You can talk to your parents whenever you are in trouble. 在遇到困难的时候,您可以向父母求助。

这是一个含有 whenever 引导的时间状语从句的复合句。如：Whenever Susan goes to the town, she will visit her grandparents. 苏珊每次进城,总要看望她的祖父母。be in trouble 陷入困境,相当于 get into trouble, get into hot water, be in deep water, run into trouble, run into difficulties。

4. Drills　句型操练

（1）look ＋ *adj.*

He looks blue now.

He looks sad this morning.

He looks depressed at the moment.

（2）feel like ...

Do you feel like walking there with me?

They made me feel like one of their family members.

Look at these words you wrote whenever you feel like smoking.

（3）... age ...

Frank is the same age as me.

He started playing the piano at an early age.

At our age, there is nothing more important than good health.

5. Recitation　常用句背诵

（1）I don't think she would do such a thing.　我觉得她不会做那样的事。

（2）Who can I turn to in my hour of need like this?　在这种需要帮助的时候,我能向谁求助呢?

（3）And your friend is someone you can turn to when your spirits need a lift.　在您的精神需要鼓舞时,您可以向朋友求助。

6. Follow Up　拓展学习

Hello Sun, Goodbye Sun

If you watched the Sun all day, it would look like it moves

across the sky. But the Sun does not move. Even though you cannot feel it，Earth is turning. It makes one full turn in 24 hours，or one day. For about half of those hours，the place where you live faces the Sun. It is daytime. The rest of the time，your home is not facing the Sun. Then it is dark. So when the Sun is shining on your home，it is daytime. Then the Earth turns. When your home faces away from the Sun，it is nighttime.

你好，太阳；再见，太阳

如果你整天观察太阳，就会觉得太阳看上去是在划过天空般地移动着。然而太阳并没有移动。尽管你感觉不到，地球却一直在转动。地球转动一周需要 24 个小时，或者说就是一天。大约有一半的时间，你居住的地方是面向太阳的，那就是白天。其余的时间，你家并不是对着太阳，那就是黑夜。因此，当太阳照在你家的时候，是白天。然后随着地球的转动，当你家背向太阳时，那就是晚上了。

Ⅲ. Expressing Anger and Regret　表达愤怒与抱歉

1. Dialogues　对话

A＝Mike 迈克；B＝Kate 凯特

A：What's up? You sound a little down in the dumps.　听起来您的情绪有点低落。怎么了？

B：I quarreled with my husband last night. He is really stubborn.　我昨晚和我丈夫吵架了。他太倔强了。

A：Calm down. Shouting won't help.　冷静点儿。大喊大叫是不能解决问题的。

B：He's really outrageous.　他太过分了。

A：What happened?　发生什么事了？

B：I went back home last night. You know I was very tired. So I took a quick shower and went to bed. I couldn't fall asleep because he was there in the living room，playing his mobile video so loud. I kindly told him to turn that down a little bit. He shouted at me.　我昨天晚上回到家很累，快速洗了个澡就上床了。可是他在客厅里把手机视频开得震天响，吵得我睡不着。我礼貌地请他把声音关小一点，他却对我大喊大叫。

A：What did you do?　那您呢？

B：I shouted back of course.　我当然也冲他叫喊。

A：Hold it，Kate. You won't accomplish anything by hollering at him，right? Why not wait until you cool down a bit?　忍一忍，凯特。叫喊是解决不了问题的，对吧？为什么不等到您冷静下来呢？

B：What would you do if you were in my shoes?　如果您是我的话会怎么办？

A：Just stay cool. When you get back home tonight，tell him that you didn't mean to quarrel with him.　保持冷静。今晚您回家的时候，请告诉他您不是真想和他吵。

B：No way，Mike. I mean it's just not my fault.　没门儿，迈克。我是说，这又不是我的错。

A：I know. It wouldn't hurt much to say sorry first. And after that，you can casually mention the problem. I'm sure he'll cooperate.　我知道。先说抱歉又不会损失什么，之后您可以慢慢地和他提这件事。我相信他会配合的。

B：All right. Let me try to do as you told me.　好吧，我试着照您说的去做。

2. Words and Expressions　单词和词组

(1) anger　/ˈæŋgə/　n.　愤怒

(2) quarrel　/ˈkwɒr(ə)l/　v.　吵架

(3) stubborn　/ˈstʌbən/　adj.　倔强的

(4) calm　/kɑːm/　v.　镇静

(5) outrageous　/aʊtˈreɪdʒəs/　adj.　粗暴的

(6) shout at　大喊大叫

(7) accomplish　/əˈkʌmplɪʃ/　v.　完成

(8) holler　/ˈhɒlə/　v.　叫喊

(9) be in one's shoes　处在某人的境遇

(10) fault　/fɔːlt/　n.　错误,缺点

(11) hurt　/hɜːt/　v.　伤害

(12) casually　/ˈkæʒjʊəlɪ/　adv.　偶然地

(13) mention　/ˈmenʃ(ə)n/　v.　提到

(14) cooperate　/kəʊˈɒpəreɪt/　v.　合作

3. Tips and Notes　要点解释

(1) You sound a little down in the dumps.　听起来您的情绪有点低落。

sound是一个连系动词,译为听起来。如：It sounds great.　这听起来很棒。又如：She sounded a bit worried.　她听起来有点焦虑不安。

(2) Shouting won't help.　大喊大叫是不能解决问题的。

Shouting是动名词,作主语。动名词作主语通常表达一种抽象的动作概念,即泛指某种行为或动作。如：Skating on real ice is great fun.　在真冰上溜冰非常有趣。Smoking is harmful to your health.　吸烟对健康有害。

（3）Why not wait until you cool down a bit?　为什么不等到您冷静下来呢?

本句也可以表达为: Why don't you wait until you cool down a bit? 句中 Why not + v.的意思是"为何不做某事"。这个句型中 not 后跟动词原形,有鼓励某人去做某事的意思。如: Why not call her at once?　为什么不立刻给她打电话呢? Why not go swimming together?　为什么不一起去游泳呢?

4. Drills　句型操练

（1）quarrel with … /have a quarrel with … /have a fight with …

You may lose your friends if you quarrel with them all the time.

He had a quarrel with his girlfriend yesterday.

We have never had a fight with each other.

（2）take a quick shower/have a quick shower/shower quickly

Why not make some eggs, toast and coffee while I take a quick shower?

We can have a quick shower instead of a bath because having a bath can waste a lot of water.

After showering quickly, I began to eat my breakfast.

（3）fall asleep/go to sleep/get to sleep/be asleep/sleep

Ask yourself, "If I were to go to bed now, how quickly could I fall asleep?"

The baby is asleep, don't make any noise wake her.

I couldn't sleep because of the noise.

5. Recitation　常用句背诵

（1）Shouting won't help.　大喊大叫是不能解决问题的。

（2）I kindly told him to turn that down a little bit.　我礼貌地请他把声音关小一点。

（3）What would you do if you were in my shoes?　如果您是我的话会怎么办？

（4）It wouldn't hurt much to say sorry first.　先说抱歉又不会损失什么。

（5）Let me try to do as you told me.　我试着照您说的去做。

6. Follow Up　拓展学习

An Apology

A＝David 大卫；B＝Kate 凯特

A：I didn't know I had hurt your feelings. My apologies.

B：Actually，I also owe you an apology. It's not all your fault. I'm to blame too. I had given you so much pressure.

A：But I shouldn't have been so rude to you. I feel horrible after yelling at you.

B：It doesn't matter. People are easy to get mad when they are too much tired.

A：Thanks for your understanding. So … are you good now?

B：Well，if you promise you'll not do it again，then yes，we are good.

道歉

A：我不知道我伤害了您的感情。我向您道歉。

B：实际上，我也欠您一个道歉。这不完全是您的错。我也该受责备。我给过您这么多的压力。

　　A：但我不该对您这么粗鲁。对您大声咆哮让我感到很羞愧。

　　B：没关系。人在疲惫时总是很容易发火。

　　A：谢谢您的理解。那么，您现在心情好些了吗？

　　B：嗯，如果您保证不再那样做了，我们就和好如初吧。

Unit 12　Attending Dinner Party
应邀就餐

Ⅰ. Dress Code　服饰要求

1. Dialogues　对话

A＝Tom，a foreign friend of Mr. Li 汤姆，李先生的一位外国朋友；B＝Mr. Li，a Chinese 李先生，一位中国人

A：Hi，Mr. Li！Haven't seen you for a long time. When did you come to America?　您好，李先生！好久不见。您什么时候来美国的？

B：Hi，Tom！I came to see my daughter here last week. Could you tell me something about dress code? Because I will attend my daughter's classmate's party next Sunday.　您好，汤姆！我上个星期来美国看望我的女儿。您能告诉我一些有关服饰要求的事吗？因为下周日我要出席我女儿同学举办的晚会。

A：OK. Firstly，follow the dress code and dress in a suitable way. Secondly，take off your hat and coat after entering the door. Thirdly，men should always wear a suit and a tie. Fourthly，men and women should not wear sunglasses indoors. Fifthly，men should shave themselves and cut their nails short.　好的。第一，遵照服饰要求，穿着得体。第二，进门后摘掉帽子，脱下外套。第三，男

154

士应着西装打领带。第四,在室内不要戴墨镜。第五,男士应该刮胡子并剪短指甲。

B：I see. Thank you. 我明白了,谢谢。

2. Words and Expressions 单词和词组

(1) foreign /ˈfɒrɪn/ *adj*. 外国的

(2) take off 脱下

(3) sunglasses /ˈsʌnɡlɑːsɪz/ *n*. 太阳镜,墨镜

(4) shave /ʃeɪv/ *v*. 刮胡子

(5) nail /neɪl/ *n*. 指甲

3. Tips and Notes 要点解释

(1) dress code 服饰要求

相当于 code of dress,rules about what to wear, dress requirements 衣着规定。

(2) cut their nails short 剪短指甲

cut 是动词,their nails 是宾语,short 是形容词作宾语 their nails 的补足语。类似的表述有：Let the boy alone. 让那个男孩独自待着。Keep the room clean. 保持房间整洁。Make our country more beautiful. 使我们的祖国更加美丽。

4. Drills 句型操练

(1) Could you ...

Could you tell me the way to the nearest hospital?

Could you repeat what you said?

Could you turn down the music?

(2) in a ... way

We should get along with each other in a friendly way.

He feels the story in a gentle way.

I like to read in a quiet way.

(3) take off ...

Take off your coat.

When does the earliest plane take off?

Why do you take off all the drawings on the wall?

5. Recitation　常用句背诵

(1) Could you tell me something about dress code?　您能告诉我一些有关服饰要求的事吗?

(2) Firstly, follow the dress code and dress in a suitable way.　第一,遵照服饰要求,穿着得体。

6. Follow Up　拓展学习

Relaxing at Home

A＝Mike 迈克；B＝Jane 简

(Mike is just back home from work. Jane, his wife is talking to him.)

A：I'm home, sweetie.

B：Welcome back, honey.

A：I'm tired. Get me a cup of beer, OK?

B：Why don't you take a shower? Put on something loose. It will make you feel relaxed.

A：A good idea. I'm going to take a shower.

B：And I bought a new pair of pajamas for you this afternoon.

A：Really? Are they made of cotton? I'm comfortable with cotton pajamas.

B：Of course, they are.

A：Great. Thank you, Dear.

在家休息放松

（迈克刚下班回家。他的妻子简正在与他交谈。）

A：亲爱的,我回来了。

B：亲爱的,欢迎回家。

A：我累了。给我倒一杯啤酒,好吗?

B：为什么不冲个澡呢? 穿上宽松的衣服会让您感到放松。

A：好主意。我先冲个澡。

B：今天下午我给您买了一套新睡衣。

A：真的吗? 它们是全棉的吗? 穿上全棉的睡衣让我感觉很舒服。

B：当然啦。

A：太棒了,谢谢亲爱的。

Ⅱ. Table Manners 餐桌礼仪

1. Dialogues 对话

A＝Mr. Li 李先生；B＝Tom 汤姆

A：Tom，would you please tell me something about table manners in your country? 汤姆,您能告诉我一些有关美国餐桌礼

仪的事吗？

B：I'm glad to. Table manners are very important. Here are the tips for you. 我很乐意。餐桌礼仪非常重要，尤其要注意以下几点。

（1）Be on time. 请准时。

（2）Do bring a bottle of wine or a box of chocolate or some flowers. 请带一瓶葡萄酒、一盒巧克力或一些花。

（3）As soon as you are seated，unwrap your napkin and place it on your lap. 当您就座时，请展开您的餐巾放在膝盖上。

（4）If you need to leave the table，you may leave the napkin on your chair and say "Excuse me". 如果您要离开，请将餐巾放在椅子上并说一声"不好意思"。

（5）When the meal is finished，place your napkin at the left of your plate. 宴会结束时，请将餐巾放在盘子的左边。

（6）Never rest your elbows on the table and silence your mobile phone. 请不要将肘部放在桌子上并将手机静音。

（7）Before dinner，the man should pull out the chair for the woman beside. 在就餐前，男士应为身边的女士拉开椅子。

（8）It's rude to whisper with the person beside you all the time. 一直和坐在您身边的人窃窃私语是不礼貌的行为。

（9）It's polite to listen carefully while others are talking. 在他人讲话时注意倾听是有礼貌的行为。

（10）Dishes are passed from left to right and finish eating all the food on your plate. 菜肴从左往右传，请将自己盘子里的菜肴吃完。

（11）Never talk with your mouth full. 嘴巴里有食物时请不要讲话。

（12）Say "Cheers" or "Here's to your health" when toasting with your friends.　与朋友祝酒时说"干杯"或"为您的健康干杯"。

（13）Before saying goodbye to the host and hostess，guests should say something grateful to them for their dishes and so on.　与男主人、女主人告别前，客人要对主人的菜肴等表示感谢。

A：It's useful for me to know table manners. It seems different countries have different cultures. Thanks a lot.　了解这些餐桌礼仪对我很有用。看来不同的国家有不同的文化。谢谢。

2. Words and Expressions　单词和词组

（1）seat　/siːt/　*v*.　使……坐下

（2）unwrap　/ʌnˈræp/　*v*.　打开

（3）napkin　/ˈnæpkɪn/　*n*.　餐巾

（4）lap　/læp/　*n*.　膝盖

（5）elbow　/ˈelbəʊ/　*n*.　肘部

（6）rude　/ruːd/　*adj*.　无礼，粗鲁的

（7）whisper　/ˈwɪspə/　*v*.　窃窃私语

（8）polite　/pəˈlaɪt/　*adj*.　有礼貌的

（9）toast　/təʊst/　*vt*.　敬酒

（10）hostess　/ˈhəʊstɪs/　*n*.　女主人

3. Tips and Notes　要点解释

（1）Do bring a bottle of wine or a box of chocolate or some flowers.　请带一瓶葡萄酒、一盒巧克力或一些花。

此处的 do 发挥强调作用。对谓语动词的强调仅有三个单词可以使用，它们是 do、does、did。如：Do come on time.　请务必准时

到。He does study very hard. 他学习确实很努力。We did finish the work yesterday. 我们确实昨天就完成了这项工作。

（2）be seated　就座

与 sit down 相比较，be seated 表达更正式、更客气一些。类似的表述有：take a seat，have a seat. 如：Do not sit down at table until the women present are seated. 入席时等女客人全都坐下后才可就座。Take a seat and make yourself comfortable. 找个座位坐下，让自己舒服一点。

（3）Dishes are passed from left to right. 菜肴从左往右传。

from left to right 意为从左往右。from ... to ... 意为"从……到……"。类似的短语有：from A to Z，自始至终。常用的短语有：from bad to worse 越来越糟，from morning to night 从早到晚，from house to house 挨家挨户，from mouth to mouth 口口相传。

4. Drills　句型操练

（1）as soon as ... /the moment/hardly ... when

It was raining as soon as I got home.

Telephone me the moment you get the results.

Hardly had he arrived when it began to snow heavily.

（2）If ...

If it rains，we'll stay at home.

Would you mind if I open the window?

Taste the soup and add some salt if necessary.

（3）before ...

Get out before I call the police.

You have to pass a test before you get a licence.

He spent his early life in China before moving to Canada.

5. Recitation　常用句背诵

（1）Do bring a bottle of wine or a box of chocolate or some flowers.　请带一瓶葡萄酒、一盒巧克力或一些花。

（2）Never rest your elbows on the table and silence your mobile phone.　请不要将肘部放在桌子上并将手机静音。

（3）Say "Cheers" or "Here's to your health" when toasting with your friends.　与朋友祝酒时说"干杯"或"为您的健康干杯"。

（4）It seems different countries have different cultures.　看来不同的国家有不同的文化。

6. Follow Up　拓展学习

Having a Western Meal at a Restaurant

A＝Jim 吉姆；B＝Waitress 女服务员

A：I think I would like to have a tomato sausage soup first. And the same for her, please.

B：Yes. And what would you like to drink?

A：One goblet of red wine and one bottle of beer, please.

B：Would you like a dessert?

A：What special kind of dessert do you have?

B：Lemon pie, hot cake in syrup, chocolate sundae and custard pudding.

A：I think we'll order after finishing the main course.

B：All right. I'll bring your soup right away.

在饭店里用西餐

A：我想先要一份番茄烤肠汤。请给她也来一份吧。

B：好的。您想喝点什么？

A：一杯红酒和一瓶啤酒。

B：您想来点甜品吗？

A：你们有什么特别的甜品吗？

B：柠檬派、糖浆热蛋糕、巧克力圣代和奶油布丁。

A：我们吃完主菜后再点这些吧。

B：好的，我马上给你们上汤。

Ⅲ. Saying Goodbye 告别用语

1. Dialogues 对话

A＝Mr. Li 李先生；B＝Tom 汤姆

A：How should I say goodbye to the host as the meal is finished，Tom?   汤姆，当宴会结束时，我该如何与主人道别？

B：It's an easy problem. You may say like this as usual.   这个问题很容易。您通常可以这样说。

（1）Thank you again for your kind invitation. It is a good night with such nice restaurant，delicious dishes and fine service. Goodbye.   再次感谢您的盛情邀请。这真是一个美好的夜晚，有这么好的餐厅、美味的菜肴和优质的服务。再见。

（2）If you think the chef is cooking well，please invite him to the table，saying "Qingqing" in Chinese and give him two glasses of wine as a token of appreciation.   如果您觉得大厨菜烧得不错，可以邀请大厨到餐桌上来并用中文说"请请"，敬他两杯酒以表谢意。

（3）Thank you for inviting us to dinner. I have a good time here with your hospitality.　谢谢您邀请我参加宴会。您的盛情款待使我在这里过得很愉快。

（4）Before saying goodbye to you，it's time for me to invite you and your family to be our guests next Sunday evening.　在说再见前，我想请您和您的家人在下周日晚上来我家做客。

A：Tom，I have learned a lot from your speaking. Thank you very much.　汤姆，您的话让我获益匪浅。非常感谢。

2. Words and Expressions　单词和词组

（1）meal　/miːl/　n.　一餐饭，一顿饭

（2）as usual　像往常一样，照例

（3）invitation　/ɪnvɪ'teɪʃ(ə)n/　n.　邀请

（4）service　/'sɜːvɪs/　n.　服务

（5）chef　/ʃef/　n.　大厨

（6）token　/'təʊkən/　n.　象征

（7）appreciation　/ə,priːʃɪ'eɪʃ(ə)n/　n.　感谢

（8）as a token of appreciation　以表谢意

（9）dinner　/'dɪnə/　n.　晚宴，宴会

（10）hospitality　/hɒspɪ'tælɪtɪ/　n.　好客，款待

3. Tips and Notes　要点解释

（1）as the meal is finished 当宴会结束时，as a token of appreciation 以表谢意

两个短句中，as 的语法功能和中文译义是不一样的。as the meal is finished 中的 as 是连词，译为"当……时"。如：All the students' eyes were on the new teacher as she came into the classroom.　当新老师走进教室时,所有学生的目光都集中在她身上。而 as a token of appreciation 中的 as 是介词,译为"作为……"。如：You can take that glass as a small pretty vase.　您可以把那个玻璃杯当作一个小小的、精致的花瓶。

（2）fine service　优质的服务

常见的短语有：good service　良好的服务、bad service　糟糕的服务、complete service　完整的服务。

（3）have a good time　过得很愉快

类似的短语有：have a happy time, have a nice time, have a wonderful time, have a great time, have a pleasant time, have fun, enjoy oneself。

4. Drills　句型操练

（1）as usual

I sat at my desk happily as usual.

As usual, we'd like to hear your opinion.

Today is my birthday, I shall be celebrating it as usual, with my family.

（2）a glass of … /… glasses of …

I can have three glasses of beer.

He drinks five glasses of water every day.

It's necessary for me to have two glasses of wine a day.

（3）It's time …

It's time for lunch.

It's time to wake up.

It's about time for us to go to school.

5. Recitation　常用句背诵

（1）It is a good night with such nice restaurant，delicious dishes and fine service.　这真是一个美好的夜晚，有这么好的餐厅、美味的菜肴和优质的服务。

（2）I have a good time here with your hospitality.　您的盛情款待使我在这里过得很愉快。

（3）It's time for me to invite you and your family to be our guests next Sunday evening.　我想请您和您的家人在下周日晚上来我家做客。

6. Follow Up　拓展学习

Exchanging Food

A＝Anna 安娜；B＝waiter 男服务员

A：What is this? I didn't order that.

B：I am terribly sorry. May I have your order again? I'll get it right away.

A：I've ordered savory pork and coleslaw.

B：I'm sorry. I must have made a mistake. I'll bring them for you at once.

（A few minutes later）

A：Hey，what is this?

B：Pardon me，Miss. But didn't you order chicken soup?

A：Oh，is that what it is?

B：If it really bothers you，I'll replace it for you.

A：No，don't replace it. Give me a refund.

B：Sorry，I am afraid we can't. But you may order something else instead.

A：Oh，really? Give me a clam soup，please.

B：OK，Miss. I hope you enjoy your dinner.

调换食物

A：这是什么？我没有点它。

B：抱歉，我可以看一下您的点菜单吗？我马上把它端走。

A：我点了美味的猪肉和凉拌卷心菜。

B：对不起，我一定是弄错了。我立刻给您送来。

（几分钟后）

A：嘿，这是什么？

B：不好意思，您没有点这份鸡汤吗？

A：哦，这是我点的那道汤吗？

B：如果它使您感到不妥，我将为您换掉它。

A：不，不用换。我要退款。

B：不好意思，我们不能给您退款。您可以再点其他菜品替代。

A：喔，真的吗？那就请上一份蛤蜊汤吧。

B：好的，女士，希望您用餐愉快。

Unit 13 Communicating with Others 与人交往

手机扫码
听单词和对话

Ⅰ. Self-introduction 自我介绍

1. Dialogues 对话

A＝Teacher 教师；B＝Li Ping 李平

A：Hi，everybody. Let's begin our topic "Self-introduction". Li Ping，it's your turn to say something about yourself. 大家好! 我们开始主题演讲"自我介绍"。李平，轮到您来自我介绍了。

B：Good morning，teachers and my fellow students. My name is Li Ping. I come from Nanjing，China. I have a happy family. They are my wife，my son，my daughter-in-law，my grandson and I. I've always been interested in English，and have worked very hard at it in Jinling University for Senior People. I spent five years learning English there after I was retired. I got high marks there and was a top student in my class. However，the more I have learned，the more I realize that my knowledge about western culture is limited. 老师们,同学们,早上好,我叫李平。我来自中国南京,有一个幸福的家庭。成员有我的妻子、我的儿子、我的儿媳、我的孙子和我。我一直对英语很感兴趣。退休后,我在金陵老年大学学了五年的英语。我成绩优异,是班上的尖子生。然而,我学得越

多,越觉得自己对西方文化了解不够。

I think I still need more practice to apply what I've learned in the classroom. So I decided to live with my son's family in the United States of America. Now I attend the advanced English class at Columbia University, which I believe it is the ideal place for me to get what I need. I hope that I can do a good job in my Western culture research. 我认为我还需要在实践中多应用课堂所学。因此,我决定来到美国和儿子一家生活在一起。现在,我在哥伦比亚大学深造,我相信这是一所理想的学府,能让我得到我所需要的东西,也希望我能更好地理解西方文化。

This is my first time in the U.S. and also my first time studying with so many foreign friends. I hope we will get along well with each other. Thank you. 这是我第一次来到美国,也是我第一次和这么多外国朋友一起学习。我希望我们能相处融洽。谢谢。

A:Li Ping told us a vivid and colourful life in learning English in China. Thank you very much. I think we'll get on well in the coming new term. 李平为我们讲述了他在中国学习英语过程中生动和五彩缤纷的生活,非常感谢! 我觉得在即将到来的新学期中我们一定能相处愉快。

2. Words and Expressions 单词和词组

(1) self-introduction /self-ˌɪntrəˈdʌkʃ(ə)n/ *n.* 自我介绍

(2) topic /ˈtɒpɪk/ *n.* 主题

(3) high marks 高分

(4) realize /ˈrɪəlaɪz/ *v.* 认识到,意识到

(5) knowledge /ˈnɒlɪdʒ/ *n.* 知识

（6）western　/'west(ə)n/　*adj.*　西方的

（7）culture　/'kʌltʃə/　*n.*　文化,文明

（8）limited　/'lɪmɪtɪd/　*adj.*　有限的

（9）attend　/ə'tend/　*v.*　参加

（10）advanced　/əd'vɑːnst/　*adj.*　高级的

（11）ideal　/aɪ'diːəl/　*adj.*　理想的

（12）research　/rɪ'sɜːtʃ/　*n.*　研究

（13）get along well　相处融洽,相处愉快

（14）vivid　/'vɪvɪd/　*adj.*　生动的

3. Tips and Notes　要点解释

（1）Li Ping, it's your turn to say something about yourself.　李平,轮到您来自我介绍了。

这句话的基本句型是 It's one's turn to do sth.　轮到某人做某事。如：It's my turn to cook tonight.　今晚轮到我做饭。

（2）I spent five years learning English there after I was retired.　退休后,我学了五年的英语。

这句话的基本句型是 sb. spends some time (in) doing sth.　某人花了若干时间做某事,其中,介词 in 常常可以省略。如：I spend too much time watching TV.　我看电视花的时间太多。

（3）Now I attend the advanced English class at Columbia University.　现在,我在哥伦比亚大学深造。

与 attend 相关的语言表达还有：attend the meeting 出席会议、attend school 上学、attend class 上课、attend a wedding 参加婚礼。

（4）I hope we will get along well with each other.　我希望我们能相处融洽。I think we'll get on well in the coming new term.　我觉

得在即将到来的新学期中我们一定能相处愉快。

get along well 相当于 get on well，意为相处融洽、相处愉快。如：She gets along well with her classmates. 相当于 She gets on well with her classmates.　她和她的同班同学相处融洽。

4. Drills　句型操练

（1）be interested in …相当于 show great interest in

All she is interested in is clothes.

Which sports are you interested in?

We showed great interest in playing the piano.

（2）the more … the more …

The more we learn，the more we get.

The more you work，the more luck you have.

The more you use the internet，the more information you will get.

（3）It is the ideal …

It is the ideal dream for us to realize.

It is the ideal place for him to learn French.

It is the ideal society for people all over the world to live in.

5. Recitation　常用句背诵

（1）I come from Nanjing, China. I have a happy family.　我来自中国南京,有一个幸福的家庭。

（2）I decided to live with my son's family in the United States of America.　我决定来到美国和儿子一家生活在一起。

（3）I hope that I can do a good job in my Western culture

170

research. 希望我能更好地理解西方文化。

（4）I think we'll get on well in the coming new term. 我觉得在即将到来的新学期中我们一定能相处愉快。

6. Follow Up 拓展学习

Introducing Each Other

A＝John 约翰；B＝Jim 吉姆

A：My name is John Smith. May I have your name?

B：Hello，John. My name is Jim White. Nice to meet you.

A：Nice to meet you，too. Where do you come from?

B：I'm from New York. What about you?

A：I was born here，California.

B：Really? This is a beautiful state.

A：It's nice talking to you. But I have to go.

B：OK. May I have your phone number?

A：Sure. It's ×××.

B：OK.

互相介绍

A：我叫约翰·史密斯。请问您尊姓大名？

B：您好，约翰。我叫吉姆·怀特。很高兴见到您。

A：我也很高兴见到您。您来自哪里？

B：我来自纽约。您呢？

A：我就出生在这里，加利福尼亚州。

B：真的吗？这是一个美丽的州。

A：很高兴和您交谈。但我得走了。

B：好的，能告诉我您的电话号码吗？

A：当然可以，我的电话号码是×××。

B：好的。

Ⅱ. Finding a Common Topic　寻找共同语言

1. Dialogues　对话

Meeting the Neighbour for the First Time
与邻居初次见面

A＝Tom　汤姆；B＝Alice　爱丽丝

A：Hello.　您好。

B：Oh，hi！　哦，您好！

A：Please allow me to introduce myself. My English name is Tom.　请允许我介绍一下自己。我的英文名字叫汤姆。

B：Glad to meet you. My name is Alice. Did you just move in next door?　很高兴见到您。我叫爱丽丝。您刚搬进隔壁吗？

A：Yes，I did. Have you lived here long?　是的。您住在这里很久了吗？

B：Yes，I've lived here for about six years. Have you lived in America very long?　是的，到现在有 6 年了。您住在美国很久了吗？

A：No. Not really. Where do you work，Alice?　不，不是很久。爱丽丝，您在哪里工作？

B：I teach piano lessons at a college. What do you do?　我在一所大学教钢琴课。您是做什么工作的？

A：I am retired now. Could you teach me piano lessons in your spare time?　我现在退休了。能否请您在业余时间教我弹钢琴？

B：Well，I'll help you with your piano lessons.　可以，我来带

您学钢琴吧。

A：Thank you very much. How can I repay you?　非常感谢。我该怎么报答您呢？

B：May I learn Chinese from you for a change? To learn Chinese and visit China are my dreams!　我可否向您学习汉语作为交换？学习汉语和拜访中国是我的梦想！

A：OK. It's a wonderful idea for both of us. I will work as a Chinese teacher then.　好的！这真是一个双赢的好主意。从此，我就要当一名中文教师了。

B：Well，Tom. Shall we start from next Sunday evening?　汤姆，我们从下周日晚上开始上课好吗？

A：All right. I'll prepare some Chinese books for you. First of all，I'd like to prepare a pair of chopsticks for you. Let's begin from the eating.　好的。我要为您准备一些中文书。首先，我得为您准备一双筷子。让我们从"吃"开始学习吧。

B：Thanks a lot. Tom，it was good to meet you.　多谢了。汤姆，很开心见到您。

2. Words and Expressions　单词和词组

（1）neighbour　/'neɪbə/　*n*．邻居

（2）next door　隔壁

（3）college　/'kɒlɪdʒ/　*n*．学院，大学

（4）in one's spare time　在某人的业余时间

（5）repay　/rɪ'peɪ/　*v*．报答

（6）chopstick　/'tʃɒpstɪk/　*n*．筷子

（7）a pair of chopsticks　一双筷子

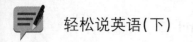

3. Tips and Notes 要点解释

（1）Please allow me to introduce myself. 请允许我介绍一下自己。

这句话的句型是 allow sb. to do sth. 允许某人做某事。如：Her parents won't allow her to stay out late. 她的父母不允许她在外面待到很晚。Smoking is not allowed in the hall. 大厅内不准吸烟。

（2）next door 隔壁

类似的表述有：next room 隔壁房间，person in next seat 邻座。如：The cat is from the house next door. 这只猫是隔壁家的。We live next door to the bank. 我们住在银行隔壁。

（3）What do you do? 您是做什么工作的?

这句话相当于 What is your job? Where do you work?

4. Drills 句型操练

（1）work as ...

He works as a tour guide.

My daughter is working as a teacher.

As I mentioned before，we work as a team.

（2）be eager for ...

The students are eager for knowledge.

It does not look good for you to be eager for leaving.

This book will be a handbook for visitors who are eager for the scenes.

（3）... since ...

She's been off work since Tuesday.

We've been waiting here since two o'clock.

It has been exactly ten years since my aunt passed away.

5. Recitation 常用句背诵

(1) What do you do? 您是做什么工作的？

(2) Could you teach me piano lessons in your spare time? 能否请您在业余时间教我弹钢琴？

(3) It's a wonderful idea for both of us. 这真是一个双赢的好主意。

6. Follow Up 拓展学习

Flying to Chile

A＝Friend A 朋友 A；B＝Friend B 朋友 B

A：Guess what!

B：What?

A：I'm eligible to study abroad next month.

B：Really? Where to go?

A：To Chile，to help build communities and learn about their culture.

B：That sounds incredible!

A：It is，but I'm worried I won't be able to get my visa.

B：Don't worry. The school will help you with those things.

A：I need to get my visa so I can fly to Chile.

B：You should probably find that out.

A：Well，I do know it costs a hundred dollars.

B：How about visa?

A：I have to apply for it，but I'm not too worried about it.

B：Well，I wish you luck，man. I'm gonna miss you.

A：I'll miss you，too.

飞往智利

A：猜猜看！

B：猜什么？

A：下个月我就有留学资格了。

B：真的吗？到哪儿去留学？

A：去智利，帮助建立社区并学习他们的文化。

B：这听起来令人难以置信。

A：是的，但我有点儿担心拿不到签证。

B：不用担心，学校会帮您的。

A：我需要签证，这样我才能飞往智利。

B：您应该了解清楚。

A：嗯，我只知道这需要一百美元。

B：那么，签证呢？

A：我还得申请，但我不太担心这件事。

B：祝您好运，伙计。我会想您的。

A：我也会想您的！

Ⅲ. Do as the Romans Do　入乡随俗

1. Dialogues　对话

Rio Carnival　里约热内卢狂欢节

A＝Friend A 朋友 A；B＝Friend B 朋友 B

A：I'm doing something amazing. I'm going to the Rio Carnival!　我要去参加里约热内卢狂欢节了，这真令人兴奋。

B：You're so lucky. It's the world's famous street party.　您太幸运了。这可是世界上有名的街道盛装游行聚会。

A：Yes，millions of people come from everywhere and it goes on for several days. The best part is called "The Sambodromo Parade". It is a 700-metre long street surrounded by spectator stands and luxury boxes which are filled with over 60,000 people. Tickets are expensive and sell out quickly.　是的，来自世界各地成千上万的人都会来参加，活动要持续几天。最精彩的部分是"桑巴大道游行"。桑巴大道是一条长 700 米的街道，周围有观礼台和豪华包厢，能容纳 6 万多人。门票虽贵，但很快就卖光了。

B：You had better get your tickets early. I heard it's famous for people dancing the samba and goes on all night.　您最好早点买到票。我听说这条街道之所以有名是因为人们在那里跳桑巴舞，而且是彻夜舞蹈。

A：Yes. And do you know there should be lots of delicious food? Because in the following 40 days after the Carnival，the local people don't eat meat. So when in Rome，do as the Romans do. During Carnival time they eat everything!　是的。您知道那里有许多美食吗？因为狂欢节后，当地人 40 天之内都不吃肉。这就是入乡随俗。狂欢节期间，他们什么都吃。

B：How many days does it last?　这个活动要持续多少天？

A：From Saturday to Wednesday.　从周六到（下个）周三。

B：Oh，so is Tuesday known as Mardi Gras?　哦，所以星期二就是我们所知道的大斋期前的狂欢节吧？

A：Yes，it means "Fat Tuesday". So that should be a clue about the food!　是的，它的意思是"肥美的星期二"，从这个称呼就能理解那些美食了！

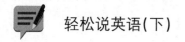

2. Words and Expressions　单词和词组

(1) Roman　/ˈrəʊmən/　*n*.　罗马人

(2) carnival　/ˈkɑːnɪv(ə)l/　*n*.　狂欢节

(3) amazing　/əˈmeɪzɪŋ/　*adj*.　令人惊异的

(4) million　/ˈmɪljən/　*n*.　百万

(5) several　/ˈsevrəl/　*adj*.　几个，一些

(6) the Sambodromo Parade　桑巴大道游行

(7) spectator　/spekˈteɪtə(r)/　*n*.　观众，观看者

(8) stands　/stændz/　*n*.　看台

(9) spectator stands　观礼台

(10) luxury　/ˈlʌkʃərɪ/　*n*.　奢华、豪华

(11) luxury boxes　豪华包厢

(12) delicious　/dɪˈlɪʃəs/　*adj*.　美味的

(13) Rome　/rəʊm/　*n*.　罗马

(14) Mardi Gras　/ˌmɑːdɪˈɡrɑː/　大斋期前的最后一天

(15) clue　/kluː/　*n*.　线索，提示，理解

3. Tips and Notes　要点解释

(1) I'm doing something amazing.　这真令人兴奋。

这里的 amazing 作为后置定语修饰前面的不定代词 something。表示"人"的不定代词包括：someone、somebody、anyone、anybody、everyone、everybody、no one、nobody。表示"物"的不定代词包括：something、anything、everything、nothing。如：Is there anything special in today's newspaper?　今天的报纸上有什么特别的新闻吗？Does anyone else want to speak at the meeting?　会上还有其他人想发言吗？

（2）millions of 数以百万计的

类似的表述有：billions of 数以亿计的、thousands of 数以千计的、hundreds of 数以百计的、dozens of 几十、a dozen of 一打（12个）。

（3）It is a 700-metre long street surrounded by spectator stands and luxury boxes which are filled with over 60,000 people. 桑巴大道是一条长 700 米的街道,周围有观礼台和豪华包厢,能容纳 6 万多人。

这是一个复合句,其中的"surrounded by spectator stands and luxury boxes"是过去分词短语作定语修饰前面的"street","which are filled with over 60,000 people"是定语从句修饰前面的先行词"spectator stands and luxury boxes"。先行词为"物"时,定语从句中的关系代词用"that"或者"which"。如：This is Lily's seat which/that is next to me. 这就是坐在我旁边的莉莉的座位。

4. Drills 句型操练

（1）be filled with 相当于 be full of

Her heart is filled with love.

We are filled with joy in our success.

My workplace is full of flowers and plants that I need.

（2）in the following ...

We'll discuss it in the following days.

He worked even harder in the following years.

In the following articles we can see our life has improved.

（3）be known as ...

Nanjing is known as Stone City.

Nancy was well known as an excellent dancer.

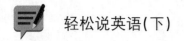

Disneyland Park was created by Walt Disney who is known as Father of Mickey Mouse.

5. Recitation   常用句背诵

(1) I'm going to the Rio Carnival!   我要去参加里约热内卢狂欢节了。

(2) I heard it's famous for people dancing the samba and goes on all night.   我听说这条街道之所以有名是因为人们在那里跳桑巴舞,而且是彻夜舞蹈。

(3) When in Rome, do as the Romans do.   入乡随俗。

6. Follow Up   拓展学习

Selling Things on eBay

A＝Friend A 朋友 A；B＝Friend B 朋友 B

A：Do you know how to sell things on eBay?

B：I've done it a few times. What do you want to sell?

A：Mostly some old games and movies. Can you help me out?

B：Sure. First you should take a few pictures of what you're trying to sell.

A：OK, you should probably help me out with that.

B：Sure thing.

A：Do they have instructions on the rest after I make an account?

B：Yeah, it's pretty simple. What do you need to sell stuff for?

A：I want some extra cash to buy books off of Amazon.

B：(laughing) So you're selling on one site and buying on

another?

A：You know me，I like to live on the edge.

在易趣网上卖东西

A：您知道怎么在易趣网上卖东西吗?

B：我卖过几次。您想卖什么?

A：主要是一些老的游戏和电影。您能帮我吗?

B：当然可以。首先,您应该给您要卖的东西拍几张照片。

A：好的,您应该能帮我一下。

B：当然可以。

A：在我开通账户后,他们有关于剩下款项的指示吗?

B：是的,它非常简单。您卖东西到底是为了什么?

A：我需要一些额外的现金去亚马逊买书。

B：(大笑)所以您在一个网站上卖东西而在另一个网站上买东西?

A：您懂的,我喜欢"紧张刺激"的生活。

Unit 14   Seeking Local Tour Information
获取当地旅游信息

Ⅰ. At Tourist Information Center   在游客信息中心

1. Dialogues   对话

A＝Clerk 接待员；B＝Tourist 游客

A：Kia ora. Welcome to tourist information center.   您好，欢迎来到游客信息中心。

B：Kia ora! We are independent travellers from China.   您好，我们是来自中国的自由行游客。

A：I see. Welcome to New Zealand.   我了解了。欢迎你们来到新西兰。

B：Do you have any information materials about the close-by tourist attractions or relevant maps?   你们有附近旅游景点的资料或相关地图吗？

A：Yes，we do. Here is a map of the scenic spots，tour facilities and public services of the whole hot spring region.   有的。这是一张整个温泉地区的地图，包含各个景点、旅游设施和公共服务。

B：Thank you very much. Since our time is limited，would you please recommend us some showcasing spots?   谢谢。因为我们的时间有限，能否请您给我们推荐几个有特色的景点？

182

A：There are many hot springs and Maori villages in the geothermal region you can visit.　在地热区有许多温泉和毛利村落可以供你们参观。

B：We'd like to. By the way，is there any place nearby we can roam about before it is getting dark?　我们很想去。顺便问一下，天黑以前我们在这附近有什么地方可以去转一转的吗?

A：Yes. There is a geothermal park，called Lake Rotorua，just five blocks away from here. It is free for the entry and car parking. We local people often go there for a running or for a walk.　有的。附近有个名为罗托鲁瓦湖的地热公园，离这儿大概五个街区。免费出入和泊车。我们本地人常去那儿跑步或散步。

B：Anything special to see over there?　那儿有值得一看的东西吗?

A：Quite a lot. There is a huge red complex with historic significance. There are many hot springs in that park，too. Unusual aquatic weeds grow well in the hot water lakes which contain high density sulfide.　有很多呢。那里有一个具有历史意义的庞大的红色建筑群。该公园里也有许多温泉，罕见的水草在那含高浓度硫化物的热水湖中长得非常好。

B：That's very inviting.　那真是太吸引人了!

2. Words and Expressions　单词和词组

（1）independent　/ˌɪndɪˈpendənt/　*adj*.　独立的，无党派的

（2）material　/məˈtɪərɪəl/　*n*.　材料，素材，织物

（3）relevant　/ˈreləvənt/　*adj*.　有关的

（4）facility　/fəˈsɪlətɪ/　*n*.　设备

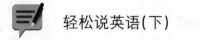

(5) since /sɪns/ *conj.* 因为,由于

(6) Maori /'maʊrɪ/ *n.* (新西兰的)毛利人,毛利语

(7) geothermal /ˌdʒiːəʊ'θɜːml/ *adj.* 地热的

(8) region /'riːdʒən/ *n.* 地区,区域

(9) geothermal region 地热区

(10) density /'densətɪ/ *n.* 稠密,密度

(11) sulfide /'sʌlfaɪd/ *n.* 硫化物

3. Tips and Notes 要点解释

(1) Kia ora 是新西兰毛利人的问候语、告别语和感谢语,其含义宽泛。它可当英语中的 Good morning、Good afternoon、Good evening、Good night、Goodbye 讲,也可当 Thank you 讲。Kia ora 是新西兰人常用的语言。

(2) Time is limited 意为"由于时间不够"或"由于时间关系"。中国人爱说"We don't have enough time",英语国家的人能听懂这句直译的话,但他们在表示"We don't have enough time"时,往往会用 Since(my/our) time is limited.

(3) here and there 是到处的意思,与 everywhere 是近义词,但前者强调"点",后者强调"面"。如:Today, KFC can be seen here and there in many big cities in China. 如今,在中国的大城市到处能看到肯德基连锁店。Beautiful flowers can be seen everywhere in the park. 在这个公园里到处能看到漂亮的花。

4. Drills 句型操练

(1) how far ...

How far should we walk?

How far can the water gun reach?

How far away can we still hear the sound?

（2）won't ... until ...

The grocery won't open until 2 p.m.

The supermarket won't close until midnight.

They won't come here until they have received your written official invitation.

（3）greet

The hostess greeted us warmly at the gate.

How should I greet Aussies when I meet them?

To learn how to greet people appropriately is very important.

5. Recitation　常用句背诵

（1）Do you have any information materials about the close-by tourist attractions or relevant maps?　你们有附近旅游景点的资料或相关地图吗？

（2）Would you please recommend us some showcasing spots?　能否请您给我们推荐几个有特色的景点？

6. Follow Up　拓展学习

Information of the Paradise Island

Come to the Paradise Island — the holiday island for young people. Here's some information for you. The Paradise Island has got two beautiful beaches. One is on the east and the other is on the west. You can make sandcastles or just sit on the chairs to enjoy the beautiful view. If you don't want to swim in the sea，you can also swim in our Olympic Swimming Pool. There are lots of things to do on the Paradise Island. There is a tennis court. You can play tennis with your friends. If you feel hungry, you can have a picnic in the forest. In the evening, you can dance at Shark Disco. There is a cinema, too. We show a new film every day. You sleep in huts at night in the Paradise Village. There is a huge gift shop, too. Come to the Paradise Island for a wonderful holiday.

天堂岛度假信息介绍

来天堂岛——年轻人的度假胜地吧！这是一些供您参考的信息。天堂岛有两个美丽的海滩。一个在东面,另一个在西面。您可以做沙堡或只是坐在椅子上欣赏美丽的风景。如果您不想在海里游泳,您也可以在我们的奥林匹克游泳池里游泳。天堂岛上的活动众多,您可以和您的朋友在网球场里打网球。如果您觉得饿了,可以去森林里野餐。晚上,您可以在鲨鱼迪斯科舞厅里跳舞。还有一家电影院,每天都会放映一部新电影。您晚上睡在天堂村的小屋子里。还有一家很大的礼品店。来天堂岛度过一个美妙的假期吧。

Ⅱ. Whale Watching 观鲸

1. Dialogues 对话

A＝Clerk 接待员；B＝Tourist 游客

A：Good morning. Tourist Information Center, how can I help you? 早上好,这里是游客信息中心,我能帮您做点什么吗?

B：Good morning. We would like to book tomorrow morning's boat tickets for whale watching. 早上好。我们想订明天上午观鲸的船票。

A：Sorry, we don't have any tickets for tomorrow. We only

have whale watching tours on every Tuesday, Thursday and Saturday in winter. Their departure time is always at 1:30 p.m. 对不起,明天上午没有船票。我们只在冬天的每周二、周四和周六才有观鲸游。时间是下午1:30。

B: Oh, we are lucky to be here in winter. Can whale watching be conducted under all weather conditions? 哦,我们运气不错,刚好冬天到这儿。观鲸活动是全天候的吗?

A: No. The tour may be cancelled due to weather or safety at our discretion. But you can have full refund. 不是的。当我们认为天气不合适或存在安全隐患时,就会取消游览。届时会全额退款。

B: Can we reserve tickets for the coming Thursday? 我们能订本周四的票吗?

A: Yes, you can. 可以的。

B: Can we reserve tickets on internet or do we have to buy tickets at the booking office? 我们能在网上订票吗? 还是说一定要到购票处买票?

A: Either way will do. There are over ten tickets available for the coming Thursday. 两种方法都可以。本周四还有十多张余票。

B: Very good. There are 8 of us altogether, including two kids. Can we buy group tickets? 很好。我们一共8个人,包括两个小孩。我们能买团体票吗?

A: I am afraid not. The minimum for group tickets is 10. How old are your kids? If they are under the age of 10, they can buy children tickets. If they are under 6, they cannot go. 不可以。买团体票起码要有10个人才行。你们的孩子多大了? 如果他们小于10岁,您可以给他们买儿童票。如果他们小于6岁则不能参加。

B: They are all under 10 and above 6. One more question. How long is the whole trip? 他们都大于 6 岁且小于 10 岁。我还想问一下整个游览的时间。

A：The whole tour usually lasts for three hours. It takes one hour to get to the blue water reserve，because those big animals only live in deep water area，away from the shelf. One hour to search for the mammals and one hour to return. So，it is around 4:30 p.m. you can disembark. 整个游览通常为 3 小时。其中，一个小时用于开往深海自然保护区，因为大型动物只生活在深水区，远离浅滩；一个小时用于寻找这些哺乳动物；一个小时用于返程。下午 4:30 左右，你们可以下船。

B：Is it certain that whales and dolphins can be seen on the tour? 游览中肯定能看到鲸鱼和海豚吗？

A：Nobody can guarantee that. In case you don't have the chance to come across either dolphin or whale，you are entitled to make another tour free of charge. 没人能保证。万一你们既没有碰到海豚，也没能看到鲸鱼，你们有权免费参加另一次游览。

B：Thanks a lot for giving me so many details about the tour. We look forward to having a memorable trip on Thursday. Bye! 非常感谢您给了我这么多有关游览的细节。我们非常期待周四的难忘之旅。再见。

A：Bye. Good luck to you. 再见。祝你们好运。

2. Words and Expressions 单词和词组

(1) whale /weɪl/ *n.* 鲸

(2) discretion /dɪˈskreʃ(ə)n/ *n.* 自由裁量权，谨慎

(3) reserve /rɪˈzɜːv/ *n.* （野生生物）保护区

（4）minimum /'mɪnɪməm/ *n*. 最小值

（5）blue water reserve 深海自然保护区

（6）shelf /ʃelf/ *n*. 暗礁,陆架

（7）dolphin /'dɒlfɪn/ *n*. 海豚

（8）memorable /'mem(ə)rəb(ə)l/ *adj*. 难忘的

3. Tips and Notes 要点解释

（1）at our discretion 意为按照我们的判断。其隐含之意是游船方说了算,游客无权决定。

（2）The coming Thursday 中的 coming 是即将到来的意思。例如,来年可说 the coming year;下周可说 the coming week。需要注意的是，coming 前面一定要加定冠词 the。

4. Drills 句型操练

（1）be lucky to ...

It is lucky to meet my favourite singer.

I was lucky to find my lost wallet.

She is lucky to find such a well-paid job.

（2）available

Jack is not available at the moment.

The ticket is available on the day of issue only.

New Zealand produced kiwi fruit is available now.

（3）due

Our flight is due to take off.

I have due cause to say that.

This book is due out in the coming September.

5. Recitation　常用句背诵

（1）Can whale watching be conducted under all weather conditions？　观鲸活动是全天候的吗？

（2）The tour may be cancelled due to weather or safety at our discretion.　不是的。当我们认为天气不合适或存在安全隐患时，就会取消游览。届时会全额退款。

（3）Is it certain that whales and dolphins can be seen on the tour？　游览中肯定能看到鲸鱼和海豚吗？

6. Follow Up　拓展学习

My Visit to Melbourne

After several hours' flight，I arrived in Melbourne，a beautiful city in Australia. The first place I visited was a small house，Captain Cook，who found Australia several hundred years ago，once lived in it. Getting out of the small house，I started my own discovery of the beautiful country. Everyone told me that the Sydney Opera House was beautiful. But I found it looked its best in the sunset when I went sightseeing by ship on the river near it. Australia is the happy home of a lot of interesting plants，birds，insects and animals. I visited a botanical garden and found that almost everything there was new to me. My most exciting moment came when I fed the Kangaroos there. They looked big and strong，but I found that they were friendly and nice animals. It was fun watching them eat！ I enjoyed every minutes of my stay in Australia，and I will never forget one little thing I have discovered there.

我的墨尔本之行

经过几个小时的飞行,我来到了澳大利亚美丽的城市墨尔本。我参观的第一个地方是一座小房子,几百年前发现澳大利亚的库克船长曾住在里面。走出小房子,我开始了对这个美丽国家的探索。大家都告诉我,悉尼歌剧院是美丽的。但我发现日落时分在它附近的河面上乘船观光时看到的歌剧院是最美的。澳大利亚是许多有趣的植物、鸟类、昆虫和动物的快乐家园。我参观了一个植物园,发现那里的一切对我来说都是崭新的。最激动人心的时刻是我给袋鼠喂食时。它们看起来又大又壮,但我觉得它们是友善的动物。看它们吃东西真有趣! 我享受在澳大利亚的每一分钟,不会忘记我在那里遇见的每一件小事。

Ⅲ. Talking about Hot Springs　谈论温泉

1. Dialogues　对话

A=Tourist　游客;B=Clerk　接待员

A: Where is the most famous geothermal park in New Zealand?　请问新西兰最有名的地热公园在哪里?

B: The most famous geothermal park in New Zealand is Wai-O-Tapu Geothermal Park, located in the North Island.　新西兰最有名的地热公园是怀奥塔普地热公园,它位于北岛上。

A: What are the main attractions in Wai-O-Tapu Geothermal Park?　怀奥塔普地热公园主要有哪些景点?

B: The most interesting attraction in Wai-O-Tapu Geothermal Park is the Lady Knox Geyser. It erupts at 10:15 a.m. every day, spraying water for approximately one hour.　怀奥塔普地热公园最有趣的景点是诺克斯夫人间歇泉,它每天上午10:15开始喷水,每次

喷水约 1 个小时。

A：How far is it from here?　它离这儿有多远?

B：It is about 80 kilometers.　大约 80 千米。

A：Not too bad. Can we see the eruption of the geyser for sure if we go there tomorrow morning?　还不错。如果我们明天早上去,肯定能看到间歇泉的喷发吗?

B：The Lady Knox Geyser erupts around 10：15 a.m. You had better get there before a quarter to ten.　诺克斯夫人间歇泉在上午 10：15 喷发。你们最好提前半个小时到那儿。

A：Is there any place we can find something to eat for lunch?　那儿有没有我们可以吃午饭的地方?

B：Don't worry.　不用担心。

A：May I ask a silly question?　我能提一个幼稚的问题吗?

B：Any question. Please go ahead.　随便问。请讲。

A：When we were driving near this city, an offensive odour greeted the nose as if we were sniffing stinking eggs. Is it toxic to health?　当我们驾车快到这座城市的时候,我们闻到一股刺鼻的怪味,好像闻到了臭鸡蛋一样。那味道对身体有害吗?

B：No, I don't think so. Native people have lived here since the time unknown. The odour comes from the sulphur contained in the hot spring water. No relevant complaints have ever been reported even if the sulphur smell is unforgettable for new comers.　没什么危害。当地人在这儿已不知居住多长时间了。怪味来自温泉中所含的硫磺。那硫磺味虽让新来者难以忘记,但我们至今没收到过相关病痛的报告。

A：Is that so! It is very kind of you giving us so much information. We really appreciate your help.　真的? 谢谢您提供了

这么多的信息。我们十分感激您的帮助。

B：You are more than welcome. If you have further questions, please phone the contact number on the foldout. Have a great time.　不客气。如果您还有什么问题，请拨打折页上的电话。祝你们玩得开心。

A：Goodbye.　再见。

B：Bye-bye.　再见。

2. Words and Expressions　单词和词组

（1）attraction　/əˈtrækʃən/　n．有吸引力的事物

（2）geyser　/ˈɡiːzə(r)/　n．间歇喷泉

（3）erupt　/ɪˈrʌpt/　v．爆发，喷发，突然发生，出疹

（4）offensive　/əˈfensɪv/　adj．令人不快的

（5）odour　/ˈəʊdə/　n．异味，怪味道

（6）sniff　/snɪf/　v．嗅，鄙视地说

（7）stinking　/ˈstɪŋkɪŋ/　adj．臭的

3. Tips and Notes　要点解释

（1）main attractions 是一个名词短语，形容词 main 用来修饰 attractions。这个短语通常用来描述一个地方或活动中最吸引人、最重要的部分。

（2）a silly question 一个幼稚的问题，与 a stupid question 的意思基本相同，后者比前者更显"谦虚"。在提问者对当地的风土人情、宗教习俗不懂或不理解但又想了解某些信息的情况下就可用"ask a silly（stupid）question"来发问。当提的问题确实犯了"大忌"时，双方都不至于陷入尴尬的境地。

4. Drills　句型操练

（1）take ... as an example

Let's take it as an example.

The teacher took Jack as a good example in the class.

The official took that poor village as a typical example.

（2）beyond

This job is beyond him.

They travelled beyond the mountains.

The landlord owns all the farmland and the buildings beyond it.

（3）chance

It is a 50-50 chance.

He has no second chance.

We chanced to meet there.

5. Recitation　常用句背诵

（1）Is there any place we can find something to eat for lunch?　那儿有没有我们可以吃午饭的地方?

（2）May I ask a silly question?　我能提一个幼稚的问题吗?

（3）Safe is better than sorry.　安全总比遗憾好。

6. Follow Up　拓展学习

Location Description　描述方位

表示一个地方在另一个地方的东、南、西、北方向,用"east/south/west/north of ..."。如:Cambridge is north of London.　剑

桥位于伦敦的北部。

　　表示一个地方在另一个地方范围内的某个方位,用"in the east/south/west/north of …"。如：Blackpool is in the northwest of England.　布莱克浦位于英格兰的西北部。Kunming is in the southwest of China.　昆明位于中国的西南部。

　　表示在某条河或者海岸线上,用介词 on。如：Glasgow is on the River Clyde.　格拉斯哥位于克莱德河畔。Chongqing is on the Yangtze River.　重庆位于长江边。Qingdao is on the coast.　青岛位于海边。

　　表示两地之间的距离,用"数词＋距离单位（如 miles、kilometers 等）＋ from"。如：Liverpool is about 30 miles from Manchester.　利物浦距离曼彻斯特大约 30 英里。Beijing is about 1,200 kilometers from Shanghai.　北京距离上海大约 1,200 千米。

　　表示离某地的旅途长短,用"a＋时间＋旅行方式（如 train journey/drive/flight 等）＋ from"。如：Newcastle is a three-hour journey from London.　从伦敦到纽卡斯尔大约需要 3 个小时的路程。Beijing is an hour's (one-hour) drive from Tianjin.　开车从北京到天津大约需要 1 个小时。

Unit 15　Talking about Life and Plans of the Old Age

谈论老年人的生活及打算

Ⅰ. Never too Old to Learn　活到老,学到老

1. Dialogues　对话

A＝Rose, a foreigner　罗斯,一名外国人; B＝Guojia, a Chinese 郭嘉,一名中国人

A：Guojia, what are you doing?　郭嘉,您在做什么?

B：I'm reading a book.　我在看书。

A：What kind of book?　什么内容的书?

B：Computer application.　计算机应用。

A：Why do you read such books?　你为什么要看这样的书?

B：Computer is very useful in my work although I'm retired.　虽然我已经退休,但计算机在我的工作中非常有用。

A：You're right. Lifelong learning is very important. Then how do you practice English?　您说得对。终身学习非常重要。那么您平时如何练习英语呢?

B：I listen to the English news besides reading newspapers.　除了看英文报纸,我还收听英语广播。

A：Your English and computer skills are much better now. I

should learn from you.　您的英语和计算机水平现在长进不少。我要向您学习。

B：It is never too old to learn.　活到老，学到老。

A：To keep a younger body and mind，one must keep learning new things. I support you.　要保持身心年轻，人人都必须学习新事物。我支持您。

2. Words and Expressions　单词和词组

（1）computer　/kəmˈpjuːtə/　*n.*　计算机

（2）application　/ˌæplɪˈkeɪʃ(ə)n/　*n.*　应用，申请

（3）useful　/ˈjuːsfʊl/　*adj.*　有用的

（4）although　/ɔːlˈðəʊ/　*conj.*　虽然

（5）lifelong　/ˈlaɪflɒŋ/　*adj.*　终身的

（6）besides　/bɪˈsaɪdz/　*prep.*　除……之外

（7）skill　/skɪl/　*n.*　技能

（8）learn from　向……学习

（9）body　/ˈbɒdɪ/　*n.*　身体

（10）mind　/maɪnd/　*n.*　理智，精神，头脑，智慧

（11）support　/səˈpɔːt/　*v.*　支持

3. Tips and Notes　要点解释

（1）computer application　计算机应用

类似的短语有：a job application 求职信、a planning application 规划申请、a passport application 护照申请、a visa application 签证申请。

（2）名词加后缀 ful（*n.* ＋ *ful*）构成肯定形容词。如：useful 有

用的、hopeful 有希望的、careful 细心的、helpful 乐于助人的、joyful 欢喜的。名词加后缀 less(*n.* + *less*)构成否定形容词。如：useless 无用的、hopeless 无望的、careless 粗心的、helpless 无助的、joyless 不快乐的。

（3）I listen to the English news besides reading newspapers. 除了看英文报纸，我还收听英语广播。

besides 意为"除了……之外（还有）"，表示"还包括某物"，同义词组为 in addition to。如：We learn singing, dancing besides English. 除了英语，我们还学习唱歌和跳舞。People choose jobs for other reasons in addition to money. 人们择业时除了钱之外还有别的考虑。

except 意为"除了……"，表示"不包括某物"。如：I like all sports except football. 除足球外我喜欢所有的运动。

apart from 意为"除了……之外"，兼具上述两种含义，应根据语境进行翻译。如：We learn singing, dancing apart from English. 除了英语，我们还学习唱歌和跳舞。People choose jobs for other reasons apart from money. 人们择业时会考虑其他原因，而不仅仅是因为钱。I like all sports apart from football. 除足球外，我喜欢所有的运动。

4. Drills 句型操练

（1）such ...

It is such a nice day!

Why are you in such a hurry?

They're such good students that we all like them.

（2）practice

Practice makes perfect.

What do you practice at school?

She practiced as an English teacher for years.

(3) keep

Keep healthy.

Keep the room clean and tidy.

I'm sorry to keep you waiting so long.

5. Recitation 常用句背诵

(1) Why do you read such books? 你为什么要看这样的书?

(2) Lifelong learning is very important. 终身学习非常重要。

(3) How do you practice English? 您平时如何练习英语呢?

(4) It is never too old to learn. 活到老,学到老。

6. Follow Up 拓展学习

Do You Like to Chat on Wechat?

A, B=Two Elders 两位长者

A: Can you surf the Internet on your phone?

B: Yep. What's up?

A: I am using a software so I can send voice messages, pictures and texts, easy and fun! Why don't you download and install it?

B: OK, I'll try. Thank you. Isn't your phone Wi-Fi capable?

A: Yes, it is. Nowadays our daily life would be inconvenient without a mobile. We do shopping, order tickets, and so on by mobile. The world is changing so fast. Everyone of us enjoy ourselves with a mobile in hand.

B：Well，one is never too old to learn.

您喜欢用微信聊天吗？

A：您会用手机上网吗？

B：当然,怎么了？

A：我正在使用一个软件,这样我就可以向别人发送语音信息、图片和文字了,简单又好玩！您为什么不下载、安装呢？

B：好的,我试试。谢谢您。您的手机是不是可以连接无线网络？

A：当然了。现在如果没有手机,我们的日常生活就会很不方便。购物、订票等都要靠手机。这个世界变化太快了,为了享受手机带来的便利,每个人都机不离身。

B：嗯,毕竟活到老,学到老。

Ⅱ. Keeping Fit and Leading an Enjoyable Life with Grandchildren
养生与享受天伦之乐

1. Dialogues　对话

A，B＝Two Elders 两位长者

A：My God! You have put on some weight lately，haven't you?　天哪！您最近发福了,是吗？

B：Not only I'm getting fat，but also I'm feeling tired. I really need to lose some weight.　我不只变胖了,还经常感到很累。我真的需要减肥了。

A：Why don't you attend an aerobic class? Or you may try jogging.　为什么不参加有氧运动班呢？或者您也可以试着慢跑。

B: Jogging? That sounds good. Jogging can keep my weight down easily. 慢跑？听起来不错。慢跑让人更容易瘦下来。

A: I do many kinds of exercises, such as swimming, jogging, public square dancing. 我会做各种各样的锻炼,如游泳、慢跑、跳广场舞。

B: What else do you do? 您还做些别的什么吗？

A: After breakfast, I go to the university for the aged to learn new things. I can learn singing, painting, playing the piano, Chinese classic poems and Chinese calligraphy there. 早饭后,我会去老年大学学习新知识。在那儿,我可以学习唱歌、绘画、弹钢琴,学习中国古典诗词和书法。

B: You are leading a healthy life. Do you need to take care of your grandchildren? 您过着一种健康的生活。您需要照看孙辈吗？

A: Yes. In the evening, I'll help my grandson with his English. Sometimes I go to his school to attend Parents' Meeting instead of their parents. 当然。在晚上,我要帮助我的孙子学习英语。有时,我还要代替他的父母去学校参加家长会。

B: How I envy you! 我真羡慕您！

A: Good health is priceless. Only if you are in good health can you do everything you want to and enjoy the life better. You can enjoy family relationships. 健康是无价的。只有保持健康,您才能做自己想做的事,更好地享受生活,享受天伦之乐。

2. Words and Expressions 单词和词组

（1）weight /weɪt/ n. 体重

（2）lately /'leɪtlɪ/ adv. 近来

（3）attend /ə'tend/ v. 出席,参加

(4) aerobic　/'eərəubɪk/　*adj*.　有氧的

(5) jog　/dʒɒg/　*v*.　慢跑

(6) public　/'pʌblɪk/　*adj*.　公开场合的,公共的

(7) square　/skweə(r)/　*n*.　广场,正方形

(8) public square dancing　广场舞

(9) else　/els/　*adj*.　别的,其他的

(10) painting　/'peɪntɪŋ/　*n*.　绘画

(11) classic　/'klæsɪk/　*adj*.　古典的

(12) poem　/'pəuɪm/　*n*.　诗词

(13) calligraphy　/kə'lɪgrəfɪ/　*n*.　书法

(14) instead of　/ɪn'sted ɒv/　代替

(15) envy　/'envɪ/　*v*.　羡慕

(16) priceless　/'praɪslɪs/　*adj*.　无价的

(17) relationship　/rɪ'leɪʃ(ə)nʃɪp/　*n*.　关系

3. Tips and Notes　要点解释

(1) put on weight　体重增加、长胖。

它相当于 gain weight。如：You have put on weight.　您发福了。反义词组是 lose weight 减肥。如：I will give you some advice about how to lose weight and keep fit.　我将给您一些关于如何减肥、保持健康的建议。

(2) Only if you are in good health can you do everything you want to and enjoy the life better.　只有保持健康,您才能做自己想做的事,更好地享受生活。

句首状语若冠以 only,通常引起局部倒装。如：Only then did I realize it was getting dark.　那时,我才意识到天快黑了。Only in this way can we learn English well.　只有这样，我们才能学好英语。

Only when you come can we start the meeting.　只有当您来了我们才可以开始会议。

4. Drills　句型操练

（1）help ...

Thank you for your help.

He always helps with the housework.

If you want another drink，just help yourself.

（2）instead of

He offered to go instead of me.

I decided to go for a walk instead of watching TV.

Instead of buying a new car，he had the old one fixed.

（3）agree ...

I agree with you.

We could not agree what to do.

Teenagers and their parents rarely agree.

5. Recitation　常用句背诵

（1）I really need to lose some weight.　我真的需要减肥了。

（2）How I envy you!　我真羡慕您！

（3）You can enjoy family relationships.　享受天伦之乐。

6. Follow Up　拓展学习

Travel by RV

Among Chinese people，a new style of living is travelling with their whole family by RV (recreational vehicle). RV are also called "Motor-homes". This means of transportation has become increasingly popular among travellers all around the world. Motor-homes are usually equipped with a fridge, a sink, an electric stove, a bathroom and beds. All your daily needs can be easily satisfied with such a vehicle so that you can travel around with no worries. The world is so wonderful that we'd like to have a good look at it.

乘坐房车旅行

在中国,人们热衷于一种新的生活方式,那就是全家人乘坐房车旅行。房车也叫"汽车之家",这一交通方式越来越受到世界各地旅行者的欢迎。房车一般都配备有冰箱、水槽、电炉、浴室和床,可以轻松满足人们的日常生活需求。有了这样的交通工具,人们可以无忧无虑地出行! 世界如此精彩,我们必须得好好享受。

Ⅲ. Making Foreign Friends Abroad
走出国门交外国朋友

1. Dialogues 对话

A＝Linda 琳达；B＝Nancy 南希

A：Good morning, Nancy! 早上好,南希!

B：Good morning, Linda! 早上好,琳达!

A：Haven't seen you for a long time. How are things with you? 好久没见了,您近况如何?

B：Not bad, thank you. And you? 还好,谢谢。您呢?

A：I am fine. Thank you. Do you come to the park every

morning?　我很好,谢谢。您每天早上都来公园吗?

B: I get up at 6:30 a.m. every morning. After breakfast, I come here to sit for a while and take in some fresh air.　我每天早上 6:30 起床。早饭后我就来这里坐一会儿,呼吸新鲜空气。

A: It is very quiet here.　这里很安静。

B: How do the Chinese people live for their old years?　中国人是怎样度过老年生活的?

A: We have many ways to pass our time after we are retired in China. Some of us stay at home to take care of our grandchildren. Others go to the park every morning as you do. In the parks, lots of elderly people do morning exercises together.　退休后,我们过日子的方式很多。有些人在家里带孙辈。有些人像您一样,每天早晨来公园。许多老人在公园里一起做早操。

B: What kind of exercises do you usually do?　你们通常做什么运动呢?

A: We usually play Tai Ji, a kind of Chinese shadow boxing. We also have fan dancing or sword dancing. Some are jogging around a lake.　我们通常打太极拳,这是一种中国的拳术。我们还会舞扇或舞剑。有些人会绕湖慢跑。

B: I think this must be a very interesting life.　我想,这一定是一种很有意思的生活。

A: Do the American elderly people live with their children and grandchildren?　美国老人和儿孙住在一起吗?

B: Usually not. When our children and grandchildren become eighteen years old, they are independent. They will have their own life and work. They will set up their own families. They should make a living by themselves.　通常不住在一起。孩子们 18 岁就独

立了。他们有自己的工作和生活,也将建立自己的家庭,必须靠自己挣钱养家。

A：We Chinese parents usually work very hard to save money just for our children's sake.　我们中国的父母辛辛苦苦地工作、存钱,就是为了孩子们。

B：We don't do that in America. But if our children get into trouble，we will give them a hand.　在美国,我们不会这样做。不过,如果孩子们陷入困境,我们也会伸出援手。

A：It sounds reasonable!　听起来合情合理!

2. Words and Expressions　单词和词组

(1) take in　吸收

(2) fresh　/freʃ/　*adj*. 新鲜的

(3) shadow boxing　/ˈʃædəʊˈbɑksɪŋ/　空拳练习

(4) fan　/fæn/　*n*. 扇子

(5) fan dancing　扇子舞

(6) sword　/sɔːd/　*n*. 剑

(7) lake　/leɪk/　*n*. 湖泊

(8) independent　/ˌɪndɪˈpendənt/　*adj*. 独立的

(9) own　/əʊn/　*adj*. 自己的

(10) sake　/seɪk/　*n*. 目的,利益

(11) get into trouble　陷入困境

(12) reasonable　/ˈriːznəbl/　*adj*. 有道理的,合情理的

3. Tips and Notes　要点解释

(1) How are things with you?　您近况如何?

类似的问句有：How are you doing? How are you getting on? How are you getting along? How are you? 如：How are you getting on at school? 您在学校情况如何? How are you getting along with your new girlfriend? 您和新女友相处得如何?

（2）They should make a living by themselves. 他们必须靠自己挣钱养家。

本句中的 make a living 意为挣钱养家。类似的短语有：earn a living，be breadwinners，earn one's bread。

（3）It sounds reasonable! 听起来合情合理!

本句中的 sound 为连系动词,意为听起来。如：She sounded a bit worried. 她听起来有点焦虑不安。

常用的连系动词中有 5 个感官动词：look 看起来，taste 尝起来，smell 闻起来，sound 听起来，feel 摸起来。如：The girl looks careful. 这个女孩看起来很细心。The food tastes delicious. 这种食物尝起来很美味。It smells terrible. 它好难闻。It sounds a good idea. 这个主意听起来不错。Silk feels soft and comfortable. 丝绸摸起来既柔软又舒服。

4. Drills 句型操练

（1）take ...

A boy takes us to our room.

He took some keys out of his pocket.

My grandparents can take care of themselves.

（2）set ...

Set the alarm for 7 o'clock.

Who set up the flag on the island?

We set off early in the morning to avoid the traffic.

（3）for one's sake

It's all for your sake.

Oh，for heaven's sake!

I hope he's told the truth for his own sake.

5. Recitation　常用句背诵

（1）Haven't seen you for a long time. How are things with you?　好久没见了，您近况如何？

（2）We have many ways to pass our time after we are retired in China.　退休后，我们过日子的方式很多。

（3）We usually play Tai Ji，a kind of Chinese shadow boxing.　我们通常打太极拳，这是一种中国的拳术。

（4）But if our children get into trouble，we will give them a hand.　不过，如果孩子们陷入困境，我们也会伸出援手。

6. Follow Up　拓展学习

Old People's Home

A＝Alice 爱丽丝；B＝Lily 莉莉

A：Good afternoon，Lily!

B：Good afternoon，Alice!

A：I'm going to live in the old people's home. I need to be looked after.

B：Why not employ a housemaid to take care of you?

A：I prefer the nursing home. The environment and atmosphere there are excellent and there are fine doctors and nurses. Besides，I can chat with many people there.

B：I see. I am sure you will be more cheerful there and you will feel better soon.

A：Will you come and see me when you are free?

B：Certainly I will.

A：Thank you，Lily.

B：You are welcome.

养老院

A：下午好,莉莉!

B：下午好,爱丽丝!

A：我要去住养老院了。我需要有人照顾。

B：为什么不请一个女佣来照顾您呢?

A：我更喜欢养老院。那里的环境和气氛都很好,有优秀的医生和护士。另外,在那里我可以和很多人聊天。

B：我明白了。我相信您在那里会更开朗,您很快就会好起来的。

A：您有空的时候会来看我吗?

B：当然啦。

A：谢谢您,莉莉。

B：这是我应该做的。